COOL IS

COOL IS

René C.W. Boender

HOT

Ambitious brain candies with a mission!

Bertram + de Leeuw Publishers

Do Not Read This Text!

Hey, why did you start reading it anyway? That's because you just ignored the word 'not'. Be sure 'not' to watch this show and the TV show will generate the highest ratings. 'Not' is strong language, 'not' seduces you, and 'not' makes you curious.

You will read a lot more about this later on. Since you have started to read anyway, I would like to thank you for buying *Cool is Hot*. Would you like to be able to carry the book along with you, at all times? Well, that's possible, because *Cool is Hot* makes excellent reading material for your e-reader or iPad, just like my bestselling book *Great to Cool*. It's about innovation, about your future, and about your new work style. It's also about your new life with *business happiness*. Just flip through your iPad if you need some brain candy, and absorb the bliss.

By the way, *Great to Cool* has become a bestseller because of the seductive technique of Dutch writer Jan Cremer. 'Bestseller' was a term he had seen on a US book cover. And it sold very well, so we'll hang on to this term for *Cool is Hot*. You'll notice that the number at the top left of the *Cool is Hot* cover is even larger! Vance Packard's 'Hidden Persuaders' do their work once again; without us being aware of it, the hidden message on the book cover has made an impact. But it's true: more than 150,000. Within 3 seconds you noticed it! What? 150,000? That is to say, by request of 150,000 keynote visitors. And now that you have bought the book too, we are firmly headed for that magical number of copies. Wow, that would be great.

® René C.W. Boender
Third edition, June 2014
All rights reserved
Creative design: René C.W. Boender
Translation: Irene Venditti, *i-write* translations and texts
Design and visuals: The Story of Brent
ISBN: 9789461560018
www.bertramendeleeuw.nl
www.reneboender.com

Wow, That's Cool! Hot, Even... | 9
It All Starts with Coffee and Trust ... | 13
Ambition Is a Must | 15
Change Is Not Difficult, but Definitely Necessary! | 18
Energy Is What We Need! So from Now on: 3"12"E(nergy) | 21
Always Keep Questioning and Chasing... | 26
Just One Job Is No Fun! Even After Retirement... | 29
Make Sure It's Hot Right Away, Otherwise It'll Never be Cool... | 32
Do You Only Look Back or Would You Rather Look Forward? | 35
It's All Moving Up into the Cloud, Now It's Your Turn! | 38
Stimulate Genius, Rediscover How to Play, and Solve It | 41
Who (Not) to Trust in Financial Maters... | 44
Try to See Things Differently and You'll See Much More... | 47
You Can See and Taste Quality, Can't You? | 50
The Shopping (R)Evolution Has Barely Started... | 53
Make Sure It Becomes 'App'ealing. It Can Be Done... | 56
Let LED Lead the Way | 59
If You Don't Provide New Input... | 62
Learn and Then Learn Some More and Be Enthusiastic About It! | 65
Listen Sooner and You'll See More .... | 68
From Globalization to Slowbalization! | 70
Chaos Equals Opportunity: The Chinese Use the Same Symbol for Both Concepts!... | 74
We Need Bridge-Builders... | 77
Become Technotolerant Too... | 80
Who Cares Where You Buy It, and When... | 84
Hope Alone Is Not Enough... | 87
Take the Stress Test, It'll Make You Feel Better! | 90
If You're Stuck, Turn to TED! | 93
Change Your Business Model and Your Outlook Will Improve.... | 95
Look It Up... and Inhale Inspiration! | 98
Stop That Passion Nonsense! | 101
The Brands & Tastes of Days Gone By, the Technology of the Future... | 104

Put That Tie Back On! | **107**
Get Clever, Negotiate Your Rent! | **110**
Music Does Much More Than Enhance the Mood... | **113**
Learn from the 'Attention Captivators'. And Absorb Their Wisdom... | **116**
Sports Heroes, Managers and the General Public Are All Addicted to SM... | **119**
The 'BB' Spirit Is Gaining Ground, Everywhere, All the Time... | **122**
Keynote, X-mas or Kick-Off Speech: Endow It with Your Soul... | **125**
Hire Dream People and You Will Again Become a Business with a Story to Tell... | **129**
May ICT Be with Us, to Each of Us His Own PA... | **133**
Apps Are 3" Door Openers. So Start Making Life Easier... | **136**
Initiatives Deserve Commitment... **139**
What Do You Do Best? Make Everything Magic... | **141**
Finding Out Too Late... | **144**
Newspapers Become Cool Again... | **147**
Chart a Clear Course! | **150**
The New Freedom: Organize More DIY... | **153**
Beware of the Social Media Blooper... | **156**
Open the New EQ Perspective and Focus on Change... | **159**
The Pop-Up Store Presents Opportunities for Innovation... | **162**
Just Do It in 24 Hours... | **166**
We're Consciously Moving from Eating Less to Eating More Often, but Tastier... | **169**
The New Travel Season Has Begun... | **172**
You Seduce People Because of Who You Are... | **175**
Hurry, Make the Big Decision! | **178**
Make the Switch | **181**
Be Brief, Make It Simple | **184**
Nowadays, Every Opinion Counts, So You Better Watch Out... | **187**
Start Pre-Selling, It Never Fails... | **191**
New Channels Are Screaming for 'Impulse' Attention... | **195**
The 'Make-Contact Media Mix' Is On & Offline... | **198**

The Rules of Impact Still Apply... | **202**
Privacy Is Becoming Piracy, So Start Managing It... | **205**
Put Pen to Paper | **208**
Headache, Migraine, or a Positive Brain Position... | **211**
The Inflation of 'Like & Endorse Me'... | **214**
Customers Have a Sixth Sense, and a Network. | **218**
We Live Longer but We Stay Younger | **221**
True Leaders Are Vulnerable and Have Guts ... | **224**
Break Through the Routine, the Grind, and the Fixed Patterns | **227**
More Speed, Service & Fun... | **230**
Will You Become a Storyteller Too? | **233**
Don't Start to Work Harder when the Going Gets Hot... | **236**
What to Do when the SM Have Turned Against You? | **239**
Copyright and the Author's Rights... | **242**
The True Meaning of Heart... | **245**
Think of What the 'Re' Can Do for You.. | **249**
Business Happiness Is a Real Privilege... | **252**
Facts, Fiction, Focus, and Above All: Fun! | **255**
Cool is Hot Glossary | **260**

René C.W. Boender

START with what is **RIGHT** rather than what is **ACCEPTABLE**

Franz Kafka

Wow, That's Cool! Hot, Even...

We are all ready for it: the New Global Optimism. Everybody wants to move on, and we've done that. The world can only be a better place if we ourselves change. And if a book is able to give you the energy and insights to do just that... then why not use it? It's really quite unbelievable: my first book *Great to Cool* has turned into the bestseller I hoped it would be. *Great to Cool* deals with hope and how to hype it! Thanks to you! Never thought it would happen, although I dreamed it would! Apparently, a lot more people are looking for business happiness, so it's really a hot topic. Not just because of the sales figures, but rather because of all the side effects it causes. My other book, *Generation Z* (co-written with Jos Ahlers), has also become the eye-opener I had in mind, aspiring to inspire entire generations. But I didn't stop there; encouraged by the success of *Great to Cool,* I went on to write *Cool is Hot,* and enjoyed every minute of it.

Thank you very much for all your support and I would like to thank the media too, for the great reviews. Such as: "Management infotainment with a mission. Write the way you talk and try to change your behavior." Each and every e-mail, what's app, and other comment I have received is very valuable to me. The compliments are wonderful, and the hard questions are food for thought. I have personally replied to each question, without exception. The questions were asked by all sorts of people, some of them famous, and who knows, maybe your question was answered too...

You start writing a book by popular request, and then you get many more requests! Finally, I know why it's called a book, because since then I've been booked for lots of speeches. So now I've written *Cool is Hot,* based upon numerous questions, and with the assistance of the 200,000 keynote visitors that have come to listen to me over the last couple of months. In *Cool is Hot* I would like to share my expertise with you once again, starting with all the various comments and questions. Because I like to talk *to* people, but not *about* them, I will not directly answer individual questions in this book, although I have used these questions as a starting point for my topics. Just like I did in *Great to Cool,* I decided to talk to you through a number of brain candies, as they are called nowadays even by well-known journalists. Brain candies are short, powerful inspirational brain twists, illustrated by imaginative quotes. Together with my creative friends at The Story of Brent I have visualized the brain candies to make them even cooler. With a bite and a sweet or bitter truth. Each brain candy is aimed at coming to mind at the moment you really need it. You can make up your mind all over again on each page. Are you going to apply the wisdom of the candy at once? Or are you going to reject the tip because you don't quite believe in it? Actually, that's where change begins: with the belief that you can and will make the difference!

Anyhow, always believe in yourself! Because the best thing you can aspire to is to become your true self. Also, believe this: the story you tell is the product you sell. People will only remember the stories, almost never the product or the deal. Enhancing your business happiness is my goal, once and for always. It's up for grabs for anyone who puts their heart and soul into their company, education, sport, or family. Coolness is the highest goal. Going from great to cool is already quite a leap, but you will only stay cool if you manage to make it hot! You will be and stay hot if people remember you and your product, and if their EQ, their emotional drive, takes over from their IQ, or rational drive. And don't forget to apply the old 3"12"Eternity rule: attract attention within 3 seconds, hold on to it for the next 12 seconds and get people to buy your product, then you'll have them captivated forever. If you manage to do this with 100% of your energy, you'll be hot!

You don't need to be a marketing expert to understand that great is just not good enough, it has to be cool. The contradiction is that cool happens to be hot. So enjoy 'snacking' on these ambitious brain candies and use their sweet sensation to make sure we're going to make the world a little bit better. Recently, I heard a keynote speech that ended with these words: "Probably, we will not leave behind a better world for our children, but we can offer better children to the world!" At least, as long as we manage to inspire the up-and-coming Generation Z...

That's our duty: yours and mine. So let's do it. Because being in business starts with giving.

Have a lot of fun reading this book, and above all, lots of happiness!

René C.W. Boender

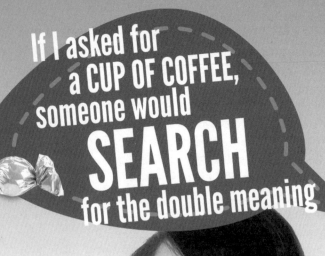

It All Starts with Coffee and Trust ...

"**W**ould you like a cup of coffee?" is one of the most frequently asked questions, since nearly everything in this world starts off with a cup of coffee. Nowadays, this might be a Vanilla latte or a popular Frappucino. "Let's discuss things over a cup of coffee" can be a great way of making contact in the business world, but also in the private dating world. By the way, the quality of a company is often reflected in the quality of the coffee they serve. Luckily, we're starting to spend more on coffee, because we realize that a fine cup of coffee is much tastier than the bland sludge 'served' to us by the ubiquitous coffee machines. The Senseo coffee pods are okay, but Nespresso has definitely helped us develop a taste for real coffee, even at home.

Coffee is currently conquering the world. And in the office, people are starting to demand good quality coffee too. The 'Walking Coffee' trend is unstoppable; there are lots of places where you can get your coffee to go. Grab a cup at Pete's coffee, for instance. And what about Starbucks, they seemed all at sea back in 2008 because of their too rapid growth. Fortunately, they've gotten back on track and they're doing great again, all over the world. Their coffee genuinely makes you want more. By now even McDonald's has discovered that good coffee makes a difference. Just taste it, it makes music in your mouth. But watch out: the competition for these coffee vendors will come from unexpected quarters. That is to say, from the banks. These days, most banking transactions take place outside the bank, so now they will try to re-establish personal contact with their clients by offering financial advice. They'll be happy to invite you for a cup of coffee, to talk things over. If you get such an invitation, don't immediately mistrust it, for once. Having a genuine and honest conversation will help us restore confidence in each other. When are you going to schedule a coffee meeting? Just do it and start building mutual trust...

Ambition Is a Must

Without a goal you will never score, without a destination you will never arrive anywhere. Of course, solid business skills will help you perform at the required level, but this won't be enough. You'll also need to possess a global mindset, as it were, a broad worldwide vision, and always anticipate on the future. Moreover, you will have to deliberately want to make a positive impact and be convinced that you can make life better and much more worthwhile than it is today.

The three Ds for the future are: Desire, Decisiveness & Determination. You'll have to get on your feet and start moving, that's all there is to it. Just keep in mind that if you never try anything, 100% of the attempts you never made will fail. It's easy to remain firmly seated and watch things evolve from the sidelines, but it's a different story if you make things happen yourself, and much more fun. One of the shirts made by McGregor sports this slogan: 'No Future without Ambition'. That's exactly the way it is. Without ambition you won't have a future.

In the future, there will no longer be any markets that sit tight, quietly waiting to be discovered. You'll have to do the work yourself, since nobody else will do it for you. And if anybody else undertakes some action, it will only be for their own gain. In the future, age will no longer be a factor that prevents people from revolutionizing things, full of ambition. Fortunately, we are witnessing an explosive growth of the number of people who are young at heart, people who want to make the world a better place, regardless of their age. It doesn't matter how you intend to do it, as long as you actually do it. Strategy 3.0 requires an ambitious perspective on the future, that is to say, a sustainable future.

Be sure to know that this means you'll need to stray from the familiar paths and be prepared to plunge into the deep, although this time they will be Blue Oceans full of opportunities. In such a world you should never be unscrupulous and there's no need

 to be bitchy; your name isn't Madonna, is it? No, it's better to be regarded as a driven, energetic manager with a clear vision. Someone who will move mountains to achieve his goals, but not at the expense of others.

What is your true ambition? What does the right half of your brain tell you right now? What do you want to achieve? Always listen to your intuition because you know that intuition is reason coupled with rush. Or, as I like to say: knowledge is fine, but make sure you couple it with swift action!

REINVENT! It's not about breaking the rules, now it's all about BENDING the rules

René C.W. Boender

Change Is Not Difficult, but Definitely Necessary!

It seems as if everyone is collectively going nuts, all at once. The world is really spinning too fast and this brings a kind of collective negative attitude with it. Almost everybody is affected by it, even the people at home. The number of divorces will rise, that's what Dutch trendwatcher Adjiedj Bakas predicts. And don't be mistaken, he is often right.

In which crisis do you find yourself at the moment, or what is bothering you? The credit crunch, the housing crisis, the euro crisis, or the worldwide crisis of nations? And to top it all off, in your spare time you have to face the baseball crisis, once the most popular sport, but no longer so! It's best not to care too much about these things.

Stop reading the papers once in a while, these doom messages won't cheer you up and you can do very little to solve these problems. On the other hand, you can clearly influence your
own surroundings. Try to avoid trouble and make sure you weather the bad times in a good way. But change at least one thing, try to break through the status quo. Because it can't continue this way, can it?

So, where to start? With yourself. Of course, everything starts with a single individual, so this goes for you too. What can you do to turn the situation around? The louder your shout for change sounds, the better it is heard. In your own head as well, your own internal voice. Start listening to this voice. And start doing this right away, bend your spirit to attain a positive attitude as an individual, start doing things! Most important, convey this attitude to your colleagues. You'll soon notice that lots of co-workers experience their surroundings as an environment where big egos outweigh good ideas, where structures and governance hinder rather than help, where mediocrity reigns, as a result of government by consent. Such a pity, because in such a world the true potential of those who wish to change will always remain the best kept secret!

That's why you need to join the battle with renewed vigor and energy. Surprise, change, and conquer. Don't be afraid to examine all of it. Rules don't always need to be broken, but you are free to bend them, you have a 'license to bend', just like James Bond, only a bit more forgiving. Push the boundaries. What can you do about it? Accept the way things are? Or see them as a challenge to become a reinventor, and enforce business happiness? Be sure to get an early start, when you're not yet under great pressure to change things. Anyone who invests more energy in their basic business DNA is by definition a winner...

The **ENERGY** of the mind is the **ESSENCE** of life.

Aristotle

$e=mc^2$

Energy Is What We Need!
So from Now on: 3"12"E(nergy)

Whoa!? Are you changing the basic rule for success, just like others are challenging Einstein's theory of relativity? Yes, definitely, but no harm done. This rule can surely be intensified, to your own advantage.

In *Great to Cool,* I explained that everything depends on the 3"12"Eternity rule. This rule makes everything more worthwhile, and above all, more fun. It's the first step towards achieving the brain status: the very limited number of brands that pop into consumers' minds whenever they decide to purchase something, also called the 'evoked set'. Set in stone in the consumer's memory. But new insights have led to further refinement of this basic rule for success. Open your mind to this, be energetic and you'll seize the 'E' for energy, and claim attention to all eternity.

Everything that has been, is past tense. All the things still to come can be influenced, by you, of course. Making contact is a matter of transmitting signals and being received. Anyway, that's what you have always thought, because nowadays things are not so clear-cut anymore. At present you can use so many different media: free social media (such as Twitter and Facebook), and paid media (such as newspapers and television networks). The starting point is still uncomplicated: attention can be earned or bought, that's still true. But by now, the online and offline worlds have become firmly glued together, and this won't change anymore. You can't live in one of these worlds without knowing and manifesting yourself in the other world as well. No contract without contact! Whether in the real or virtual world. Making and maintaining contact is important; if you can't manage this the rest is idle talk. And ideally, good contacts lead to contracts, of course.

But in practice this is much harder than in theory. What exactly should you do, and, above all, what should you refrain from doing? Generating 'Attention' (the A in the AIDA marketing model) and subsequently, 'Interest' is crucial, but it's an elusive process.

In the business-to-business world as well as in the consumer market, where uniformity and competitiveness reign. Everybody knows it works this way. But how does it work? Success begins with an understanding of the 3"12"E rule. Three seconds, 12 seconds, eternity. The beeline to making contact.

In three seconds you need to trigger the emotional PAR, the Primary Affective Reaction. In other words, the first 'yes'. In the next 12 seconds you need to seize the second 'yes', the more rational SAR, the Secondary Affective Reaction that is loaded with EQ, emotional intelligence. PAR and SAR are at the basis of the 3"12"E rule. Three seconds, 12 seconds, and as a result you get the E for Eternity. As long as consumers are tuned into you, that is. Because, unfortunately, they operate the controls and like to zap around; if you don't interest them, they'll look elsewhere and continue surfing the net. This means the three seconds are the trajectory from first contact to everlasting contract.

One, two, three. Within three seconds, the sender must attract the receiver's attention. The recipient's decision is a fast, intuitive process, where every cell in his brain cooperates in a flash. Once his interest is raised, this is followed by a somewhat lengthier, more rational 'checking' phase in which the receiver decides whether to grant you eternity. Within 12 seconds he'll check whether his first impulsive interest was justified, and if it's worth his while to explore a bit further, to listen, or even to order the product right away. If you survive the 3"12", you have the best chance of acquiring a valuable contact. In an ideal world, 3"12"E always leads to a contract, which basically is a long-term thing and forms the basis for further purchases; this customer will return to buy more. Although you will need to keep confirming this, over and over again.

Nevertheless, over the years we've gained more insight into how to prolong eternity. The more energy you invest in your business DNA, the more people will choose you. In fact, if the E stands for energy in your company, you'll always be granted the project by any customer, given that the price is right. Yes, that's right: if the price is competitive, the energy will be the decisive factor. This is what it's all about: does the man or woman making the proposal make me happy? Better still, customers are apparently willing to tolerate a difference in price of 3 to 5% and still prefer to do business with the supplier who has more energy stored in his genes, rather than listen to his whining competitor who might be cheaper, but manages to drain every ounce of energy from each and every meeting.

A very strong move is trying to combine modern design and energy in one great effort. 'D+E' may drive up the price of an emotionally charged product or service by 5 to 50%. Examples: space travel with Virgin Galactic, the new BMWs, Apple's iPod, the SENZ storm umbrella, the espresso machines made by Nespresso... But you can also find quite a few examples in the business-to-business arena, such as the DMi data mining technique which enables the authorities to quickly and efficiently anticipate dangerous traffic situations or changing weather conditions. And the same can be said of techniques that help you monitor and manage the public cleaning service in a city, or state-of-the-art software with which you can finally and easily do your bookkeeping in the 'cloud'. All these products were developed by combining the latest ICT techniques with beautiful designs that capture the imagination, and by introducing all kinds of clever utilities that save time and energy.

The A and the I from the ancient AIDA model (where D stands for Desire and the final A stands for Action) now have a time limit that lasts mere seconds. It's really true, all sorts of people – BtB entrepreneurs, consumers and CEOs alike – make up their mind in two steps that last just a few seconds. After that, they're totally prepared to tweet their decision to the world. If we arrived at our decisions in a rational manner, we'd employ a different buying strategy and spend our time in a different way. But we decide on an emotional level, with our EQ, or even our spiritual SQ. The mind is becoming ever more important; you could say that 'mind over matter' is the trend.

How is your 3"12"E build-up? Is it energetic enough, before you start claiming eternity? Does it energize you and whet your appetite? If you manage to make contact and get the other party excited, you're cool! That's better than good and great. If you can repeat this time after time in fewer seconds and prove yourself, you're hot. You will quickly take the step from Cool to Hot. Which energetic component can you add to your brand personality?

BELIEF creates the ACTUAL FACT

William James

Always Keep Questioning and Chasing...

In troubled times, managers tend to hide in a corner and ride out the storm. But as you know, accidents happen, even in your corner of the world. That's why I would advise you to go out into the open, don't let yourself be cornered. Leaders, in particular, need space. A true leader goes in search of space, or creates the space in which he can do business.

A pessimistic attitude has never done anyone much of a favor. On the other hand, an optimistic view has often resulted in good things.

Remember you've always got a choice. But you will need to be able and willing to see this, however fossilized you are. So deliberately start looking for ways to improve the situation. Please, don't spend too much time wondering why it all went wrong. There is no point, because we can't influence the past. Although... if the researchers of the CERN nuclear laboratory prove to be right, the latest test results seem to contradict even Albert Einstein's theory of relativity. In theory, we'd actually be able to influence events that happened in the past, at least if some particles are really moving faster than the speed of light. But this doesn't seem feasible in the near future. Although someone like Berlusconi would relish such a possibility, just to erase a few of his questionable assertions from our collective memory. Even so, older Trekkies were indoctrinated for years on end with the existence of the 'space-time continuum' and might still believe in manipulating history. Although Captain Janeway of Star Trek Voyager warned them off often enough: "Don't mess with the space-time continuum!"

Of course, we can manipulate the future a little. That's why you need to deliberately look for ways to improve the situation. Believe me, there's more than one way to skin a cat, even under the worst circumstances. But you need to be willing to see this. So always keep questioning and chasing. And above all, keep believing that tomorrow will bring new opportunities. Ignore the threats.

Walk towards the light and don't forget to insert the NAFTA at the end of each conversation. In the end, most people forget to ask these questions: do I get the order or the assignment, do we have a deal? Remember: NAFTA stands for NOW ASK FOR THE ACCOUNT! Who can you ask to become your customer? Give them a call and simply pop the question...

Just One Job Is No Fun!
Even After Retirement...

Everything passes ever faster, which causes people to dream about the past in order to give them a sense of preservation. Nostalgia marketing, that's what you could call it, and in fact some branding strategists actually use this term. Especially the baby boomer generation, and Generations X and Y as well, suffer from this condition. The tragic thing is, you can make a lot of money out of it. But watch out: this won't last much longer, these emotions will change tack completely. After World War II, lots of countries developed into excessive social welfare states! Anything was possible during these years of reconstruction.

Well, the kids who are part of Generation Z, the youths who are going to hit the labor market around 2020, have a different point of view. Until recently, most average citizens were born with the same kind of innate program; live through your early years, pursue an education, marry according to plan and then get a job. Usually this implies getting up at 7 a.m., having breakfast, going to work, having an uneventful and boring lunch break, listlessly sitting in front of the TV and then going to bed without a trace of passion, five days a week. Saturdays are meant for washing the sacred cow, hauling the kids around from baseball practice to football practice, and sometimes the tennis court too. Afterwards, you have to put up with evening visitors, your mother-in-law, or watch American Idol or whatever show is most popular at the time. On Sundays you can sleep late, go to church (if you're still religious), and in the afternoon visit your family or take a nostalgic trip to the zoo. And on Monday the whole cycle starts again, until at last you can retire. Then you can 'enjoy' your pension until you need to move into an old people's home or residential care. At the end of it all, you can look forward to a (too expensive) funeral or cremation, and that's it!

But Generation Z isn't going for this. In fact, they hate this kind of life. They love variation. That's why it will become a status symbol to have more than one job. Not just one job, but at least three. Working three days as an employee, one day self-employed, and another for the greater good. Just watch: senior citizens will start adopting this lifestyle too. Being a couch potato is no fun; actively doing something is much more rewarding. Generation Z and our senior citizens are much more passionate about a fulfilling job and a happy life in the here and now than about spending their old age sitting at home.

In the last couple of years, it seems all the adventure has been taken out of life by a sense of false security! Don't forget that you can do something about it. Employ young Z-people, even if they're only willing to work for you three days a week. Employ older people who still have some spunk left in them. Even if it's just for one day a week. Make sure you work with people who still have the ambition to achieve something in life! Surely that's what you want for yourself too?

A goal without a PLAN is just a WISH

Antoine de Saint-Exupery

Make Sure It's Hot Right Away, Otherwise It'll Never Be Cool...

Whenever you start producing something, you should be determined this is going to be the most wonderful thing ever made. Or the best. Or the fastest... Imagine it should make people happy (or happier). Or it should make life a bit easier. This isn't hard, unless you intend to accept mediocrity during this process; then your product will never become first class, no matter what line of business you're in. These basic principles are already established at the beginning of your career. Are you going to do something out of economic necessity? Or do you intend to do the things that give you the most pleasure...?

The initial phase of all things is important, and generally essential to the rest of the project. Right at the beginning is when it's decided whether you are going to win or lose. Just think back to the first job you ever applied for. Why did you do that? You need to like it. If you don't like it, do something else. This will certainly apply to the youngsters of Generation Z, who will be coming into the workplace in the next couple of years. They'll have a wide choice of jobs. This makes it a good idea to follow your heart and do something that really excites you. Preferably, go to work in an environment that inspires you. Maybe you'll end up with one of the big innovators. Such as adventurer Richard Branson, coffee wiz Howard Schulz or the late but great innovator Steve Jobs.

At the start of his career, Steve Jobs got excited when he read Atari's job vacancy: 'Have fun, make money'. That seemed like a good idea. But he wanted to do it on his own. That's why he preferred to work the night shift and develop his designs in solitude... later on he knew better and he started asking the crowd for advice! Working for Atari he embarked upon his ongoing quest, always looking for new items that would really make a difference.

He was stubborn and determined to carry out his plans, and not afraid of conflict. Some people might say he was a maniacal nerd. But he was a brilliant control freak who managed to design easy-to-use electronic equipment for millions of people in the thirty years he was allowed to work on his products. He always kept searching until he found it... and he invented lots of things. You can read all about it in the great biography by Walter Isaacson, simply called *Steve Jobs*. He really became 'the big inventor', with the 1984 Macintosh computer, i.e. the First Mac, and by perfecting the making of cartoons, and inventing the computer mouse. And the rest is history: iPod, iPhone, iPad, iCloud, and there's much more to come.

He hated middle of the road and mediocrity. He forced the people around him, but most of all himself, to go the extra mile. He was always pushing the limits. That's why he re-invented the computer store. He wanted it to be a place where people would love to buy things, without the manufacturer having to sell things (!!!!). We can all learn a lot from Steve Jobs! For instance, why do fashion stores often look like converted drycleaners? If you want to change this, you could ask yourself: WWSD? What Would Steve Do?

If you hear a voice in your head that says: well, just do this... Then you know what to do. And if you make this your goal, it suddenly seems to become feasible. If you only keep pondering and don't take any action, it will just remain an unfulfilled wish.

Goals are always a hassle because they tend to put you to work right away. It's downright hard work to achieve what you want. And you'll have to accept that you'll need to be very tough (on yourself) now and again.
But, try to be nice...

Do You Only Look Back or Would You Rather Look Forward?

How do you look back on the past couple of years? Which moments stand out and have put you on the right track, on the path to business happiness? Why is it always the case that these thoughts only occur to you at the end of the financial or calendar year? Why would you spend a year beating a dead horse if you're already aware that the project doesn't stand a chance? Often, you realize early on that you're driving down a dead end street and should turn around, but you keep going regardless. Could that be caused by the Christmas spirit, for example? Is that the only time we open ourselves up to our emotions and allow our EQ to decide? Everybody's busy lighting candles and adorning trees, shops and houses are decorated and the trees are hung with green LED lights that illuminate the outside world. Sure, it's Christmas and we're getting sentimental.

For me, this is a very good reason not to synchronize the financial year with the regular calendar year. Splitting up the financial year will ensure lots of attention and even generate energy at a different moment in the year. Why don't you ask one of the companies who celebrate their financial New Year's Eve on June 30th how it works? You'll be sure to get more attention from your accountant or financial advisor, because he's got more time and is willing to give you more time. But all right, the end of the year isn't in sight yet...

By the way, how's your own light doing? Wouldn't it be nice if we would all let our light shine? People who radiate light are always much more attractive than sourpusses. People who like to shine know that being in business starts with gentle generosity and emitting light. Presenting yourself the way you really are, to make the world a little prettier. No matter how big your world is, or how big you're going to make it. Believe in yourself and in the opportunities that arise, especially these days. Every single day, you can decide to make your dreams come true, and above all, to enjoy the things you believe in.

Now is the time to think these things over, rationally. Do it with your soul, because soul power is unbelievably strong, as long as you realize that everything is relative. And call your accountant and the tax office, change the end of your accounting year and

switch the date to a point in time that has nothing to do with the month of December. You'll notice that the tax collector's office or the IRS can also make things better and easier. The future is what we make it. One thing is certain: at one time or other, we are all going to die. But before it comes to that, we still have a lot of work to do...

It's All Moving Up into the Cloud, Now It's Your Turn!

Currently, we are living in a very tumultuous, ICT-related, revolutionary era. Everything is evolving and on the move at a crazy pace and things are changing faster than ever before. Kids are being trained for jobs that didn't exist ten years ago, 'homeland security' is an industry nowadays and not just something from a TV cop show.

The cloud accountant has not been invented yet, but in ten years' time it will be the hottest accountant in the world. That's right, Generation Z don't want to keep on unnecessarily doing things themselves and doing often tedious chores. They're taking things a step further, wondering whether they can do their bookkeeping in the 'cloud', on the Internet, and have the tax office check the books immediately. Crazy idea? Not at all, why shouldn't you enter all your records directly into the tax office's database, have them check things and settle VAT and taxes at once? Also, this looks like a great solution for the growing group of self-employed entrepreneurs. No more tax debts, and if your debtors are late paying their bills, the tax office will have to wait as well. Big Brother already watches everything you do, so why not include your bookkeeping?

Such a scenario would mean that taxes wouldn't need to be paid in advance anymore. And that software developers who develop online applications are going to make a lot of money. In short, anything that doesn't need to be done by people themselves will in future be integrated into digital solutions. It's incredible how many new things are being made possible by the digital revolution. In this tangled mess we're all searching for direction, based on our common sense, our intuition, or even by blindly feeling our way. Because all of these new opportunities invoke just as many questions and create lots of chances, but threats too. Questions about what is just and responsible, what makes sense and what doesn't, and what are the risks.

Naturally, for the young Generation Z this is the only world they know! With all its new means, meeting places and communities. They'll take everything in their stride and regard each new opportunity as a fact of life. After all, for these Zs it's business as usual, they aren't pampered with, but weaned on, the Internet. It's always there, anytime, anywhere. However, for older generations such a life will seem a bit more complicated. That's because they're used to a different kind of life; they have their habits, customs, values and principles. They don't just need to learn, but to 'unlearn' a lot too. Generations X and Y had plenty of experience, guidance, and certainties that made them feel secure. Letting go of these is especially tough on the baby boomers.

Yet we all buy our books online nowadays, because it's so easy. We book our trips online and even dare to travel to the airport without clutching our paper airplane tickets firmly in our hands. Why not, it's all in the cloud, isn't it? Finally, ICT is no longer a goal but a means to enhance the quality and attraction of daily life. Hopefully this will also penetrate the educational system, where they will need to develop new learning and teaching strategies. This will drastically change the system; of course many students have already taught themselves how to search the net, often with good results. But inspired teachers are a prerequisite for really instilling knowledge and letting kids experience things. The simple truth is that certain types of information can never be found by search engines – the invisible web. But not a single student knows this. With the exception of the few smart nerds who have trained themselves to be professional hackers!

In short, the cloud will make our life easier and more fun. What do you need to do to eliminate certain tedious tasks from your business and have them executed for you in the cloud? It will relieve you of a lot of stress, save time, and often be cheaper to delegate these tasks. Just ask the folks in the cloud. You'll be surprised how many people will take the time to answer your questions…

Stimulate Genius, Rediscover How to Play, and Solve It

Believe me, the world is full of good and benevolent people, who are willing to solve any problems and still dare to dream, still have wishes they earnestly want to fulfill. Just take a look at Apple commercials: the different ones. Unfortunately, there appear to be just as many people who nip everything in the bud, are very judgmental and keep suffocating things in such a way that all energy is lost in negativity and endless rounds of putting things into perspective. Generally, pessimists tend to be badly informed optimists. So it is our task to inspire them and make them experience that the glass is half full, not half empty.

The more energy you put into this, the better it works. Of course, the big question is why we always wait until the last minute before taking action. For example, look at the USA for Africa campaign; world-famous artists from the 20th century singing their hearts (and souls) out. These lyrics must have hit the paper straight from the heart. Perhaps you sang along again last Christmas when they played the song on the radio.

But did it help? Or is there still famine in Africa? Isn't it true that you often listen but don't hear anything? Except when the words genuinely touch your heart. Why don't you read some of these lyrics? They're beautiful:

There comes a time when we heed a certain call
When the world must come together as one
There are people dying
And it's time to lend a hand to life
...
And the truth, you know,
Love is all we need
We are the world, we are the children
We are the ones who make a brighter day
So let's start giving

Sadly, campaigns such as ONE, where famous artists from all over the world unite to fight famine, are still very necessary. Fortunately, more great ideas are simply begging to come true. For instance, in late 2011, Dutch journalist and former professional cyclist Thijs Zonneveld came up with the idea of building an artificial multi-purpose mountain somewhere in the Netherlands. A goofy idea? Obviously, but to be honest, it's brilliant. Plans are dull, dead reports, but initiatives generate energy and are usually halfway down the road from cool to hot. Building an artificial mountain more than a mile high in the Netherlands, suitable for housing all the greenhouses in our country. This mountain could also generate energy and you could build scenic cycling tracks through its core.

The mountain could achieve lots of things: it's the ideal way of producing food. It could provide food security once there's 9 billion of us. It could also be a way of stopping worldwide deforestation.

It all started with one of Thijs's newspaper columns and the idea started to catch on. Then some brilliant minds, equipped with the 'Yes, I can' attitude, started working together in a crowd. Builders, engineers, water managers, journalists, and marketing experts. Because after all, "the story you tell is the product you sell!" It all came together in diebergkomter.nl (this mountain will arise). Finally, a project emerged that is based on the New Global Optimism, something to make a small country proud. It has the potential to become the second best story since Hans Brinker's finger in the dike. But unlike this old story, the mountain might come true, as the initial explorations show, so let's support Thijs.

Now let's get back to your own ideas, because the ROI (Return On Idea) can often be realized as you go along. Do you already have an idea for your own business, an idea that really excites you because it's the ultimate solution for all your customers? Take a day off, clear your head and think about what kind of things you'd like to develop to make the world a better place. OK, go ahead, you may also think of something that's just for your own good...

Who (Not) to Trust in Financial Matters

Because all of the credit problems, possible liquidity deficits and new standards regarding solvability, it has become harder and harder to see the forest for the trees, to separate the wheat from the chaff. The people who cry "trust me" the loudest are often the people you can trust the least, sadly enough. Nowadays it doesn't make a difference whether you've known people personally for ages and think they'll never cheat you; there are no longer any guarantees.

Think about the numerous hedge fund scams and Ponzi schemes, all based on attracting and misleading investors. Such as the scam of sports fan Nevin Shapiro, who got all kinds of sports celebrities to invest in his chain of grocery stores which existed only on paper. But lots of people were interested in doing business with this guy, and spending time aboard his 1.6-million-dollar yacht. Or, take a look at the large number of real estate scams and mortgage frauds, such as the Sarasota real estate fraud. In that particular case, distant fake buyers bought properties with fake checks or faint promises and, after the owners had moved out, went on to sell these houses to real buyers. And what more can be said about broker and investment trickster Bernard Madoff?

These days, we urgently need stable guidance, pillars that can be trusted 100%. It's everybody's good luck that the banks will soon start taking the lead in this field again. Without the exaggerated bonuses but based on a fair trade principle, with a fair price as a starting point. Good plans and initiatives deserve to be financed; bad ideas weeded out. Also, the financial backing for these great ideas will come from different sources. You'll see more and more private individuals give financial support to cool start-ups. These are often people who have stashed their money away in idle bank accounts, in long-term hibernation and at a low interest.

If you want to invest your money in these types of financial plans, you'll always have to make sure the agreements are firmly recorded in contracts that don't leave room for speculation. In fact, you need to lay down all these terms just to be in a strong legal position if things turn out for the worst. This will prevent a lot of problems. Even if your own family decides to back you financially, it's good practice to detail and record all the agreements. Perhaps all the more so, because you're dealing with your own family. Comments such as "But I thought we agreed that..." can cause great problems afterwards, and many a family row has its roots in quarrels about money and differing interpretations of the agreements made. This is especially true if you've made a success out of your business, backed by your nice uncle. He'll turn out to be a genuine werewolf instead of a generous relative. That's because money turns people into werewolves. And it doesn't even have to be midnight for this to happen.

Anyhow, trust needs to be restored, but it's not always clear who you can or cannot trust. For this reason there will be a proliferation of all sorts of quality marks and hallmarks, which companies will start to use as a kind of logo. Like the food companies used to do, and a bit like the ISO standards in the old days. But watch out: these logos don't mean a lot. The only thing you can infer from such a logo is that the company, at some point, met the standards of the company that issued the quality mark. These hallmarks and quality stamps are pure marketing seducers. That's why it is always better to check out a company's reputation yourself, and try to find out how they handle their payments. When in doubt, just make the call yourself and don't hesitate to change the agreements if somewhere deep down inside you don't fully trust things. Don't be afraid to lose the contract, because companies that get angry when you start asking critical questions usually aren't completely above board. But companies that immediately see what you're getting at are based on solid ground. Don't forget, the promise only becomes a deal once the money has actually been paid into your bank account.

So, how many calls are you going to make to prevent being cheated, or finding skeletons in the closet? Anticipation is the key that opens the door to a better deal.

Try to See Things Differently and You'll See Much More...

If you really want to see things differently, you need to start by really wanting to change things. Don't resign yourself to the current state of affairs if you're not happy with them. Do anything you can to make things go your way. Seeing things differently, or rather, being different, appeals to your creative abilities. And you'll need a certain amount of courage because you're moving out of your so-called comfort zone. You're leaving the old and trusted path.

Once again, you're feeling adventurous, hunting for something that does excite you. Not just for the purpose of turning your prospects into new customers, but primarily to remain attractive to your current customers. The more energy you invest in this, the better the results will be. That's right, the E that stands for Energy is the best tool in customer relations. And it's also a powerful magnet for attracting new adventures, although the funny thing is, we always seem to invest more energy in attracting new customers. But you need to realize that your current customers provide your current income. They are your livelihood.

Professor Philip Kotler, the internationally renowned marketing specialist, keeps pointing out that customer loyalty is the engine that drives growth, and how very right he is. At least, if you succeed in satisfying the needs of your customers, time after time and in a superior manner. This is called creating fans, expanding your fan base, the people who like to talk and tweet about you, and appreciate your speed and great service. Prospects that have never spent a single dime on your products often get better offers and more attention. A young, successful entrepreneur told me the same after I gave a keynote talk at a very inspiring location – The *Ontdek Fabriek* (discovery factory) on the high-tech campus of Eindhoven University of Technology, in the south of the Netherlands. He put it like this: "Wanting to be different is the essential element I've picked up from this safari of ideas of yours. The power of pure ideas is unsurpassable! Transparency in networking opens up new opportunities, it makes a difference and it's nice. Personal branding is valuable and the driving force behind permanent change; commitment is a basic premise; emotion can and even must be visible; breaking through the routine is a continuous process; and inspiration is available for free and can be found anywhere, you just need to see it."

Think about it: what can you do to make your product or service truly distinctive and irreplaceable? Often, the difference lies in small things. If you're in the Netherlands, be sure to take a look in the *Ontdek Fabriek*. There, children literally start exploring their surroundings and invent things you thought you already knew.

Wake up your inner child! Come and play...

You Can See and Taste Quality, Can't You?

The **EQ of food, of anything really, is winning the battle** with the IQ. The catering and hotel industry revolution has finally been unleashed. If this weren't the case, everyone would bring along their lunch box to work, or eat at home. Yeah, right, but it's such a hassle and these things cost time. And we don't have time. So we spend our money on 'ready-to-go' convenience products made especially for us. In the supermarket or at the deli on the way home.

Of course, we're prepared to pay for good quality, but we also want to be entertained. It has to be hot to buy things there or have them delivered. Like at the Carnegie Deli in New York, the most famous in the USA, according to some. Or at Thijl's store, the grocer from Amsterdam, who is perceived as  'camp' when he delivers his organic vegetables to your door. Customers like to feel it, see it and taste it, of course. Anywhere. In restaurants too. One of America's well-known restaurant critics bases his judgment on the quality of the bread and coffee served; according to him, this determines whether the business serves tasty food (or not). As opposed to the way in which the famous Michelin stars are awarded, we may say. By serving the wrong kind of bread you can forget all about a third star in his opinion. Apparently, the devil is in the detail. Next thing you know, your customers share everything on Twitter and you'll have a hit on your hands. Really? Yes, that's the way it works nowadays.

The times of just serving a pot of coffee are over. These days, lots of people drink better coffee at home than is served in many a restaurant. If I were you, I would make sure that you serve the very best coffee, like it should be. In a preheated cup, as is customary. Just like it should be... even at work, anywhere you work. Sure enough, top quality doesn't have to be much more expensive, but it will taste much better. Serve good quality, especially if you're in the food and catering business.

Looking at the beer trade, you'll see there's a green revolution going on. Not just in genuine beer countries, like Holland and Belgium. All over the world, people are starting to rediscover the taste of beer. Heineken is really pleased with these developments; a tasty beer is always welcome. Not only men, but women too are developing a taste for the so-called special beers. So make sure there is a wide range for them to choose from, since having a choice makes people feel good. And that's what it's all about: emotions...

This goes for wine too. Offer better quality wine and you'll be rewarded with a larger turnover. By now, the wine crowd has changed a lot. They've become more adventurous. We're all done drinking ordinary red, white or rosé wine. Currently, it needs to be a Chardonnay for the girls, a classic Burgundy for the old-fashioned oenophiles, and some New World wine for the young at heart.

This is a good reason for investing more energy and enthusiasm in matters that matter: bread, coffee, beer and wine. Taste buds never lie, so make sure you make everything tastier than ever and you'll get the attention you deserve. On your fans' social media pages. You can conquer them, one by one. Every single day...

What about the taste of your bread? Does it look and taste authentic and traditional? And do your customers feel truly welcome? Or are they seen as an annoying interruption of your daily work?

The Shopping (R)Evolution Has Barely Started...

Undoubtedly, you could just wait and see what happens. On the other hand, you can also take matters into your own hands and make things happen. How would you like it to be? Whatever 'it' may be. Losers and loudmouths who start grumbling after the fact are only looking for excuses, the winners have taken the initiative and have decided to do something about it, to address matters. For instance, the shopping preferences of the masses.

In the previous century it was already predicted that the end of traditional shops was in sight. Direct Marketing and mail order shops, web shops, would take over the entire market. Actually, this didn't happen. Shopping is so much more than just purchasing items. For many people it's an outing. An addictive activity. And a necessary evil for those who don't have a lot of time. Nevertheless, history seems to repeat itself. Even the medieval peddler is on his way back.

Shops that keep abreast of the times know that this development will continue. The more you manage to accommodate your customers, the more you'll be able to affect them. So follow the trend and turn your store into a playground where people may try things out and touch anything they like. Take Apple stores, for example. Continue that practice on the Internet and sell your products at different prices, one price for nighttime buyers and another for daytime buyers, for instance. We recently tested this strategy and the turnover increased by 21%. Not bad, eh?

Yes, sales can increase dramatically. Another tip: create an 'app' to make it easier for customers to access your store through the net. The lower the hurdles, the better it works... The fewer clicks or operations are necessary, the faster the party can get going. Give the ICT cracks of Generation Z free reign to do whatever it takes. Let them build the kind of apps that can do more than just rake in your customers' money. You can even try on clothes through an app. Which you can then forward to your best friend (or lover). Such a world is envisioned by lots of global trendwatchers and trendtellers, a world in which all kinds of tasks are automated and are executed online, on the Internet. Through an app, of course, how else?

Let yourself be inspired and get cracking. Do it. Otherwise, you'll stand on the sidelines and start to lose ground, among other things. Such as pleasure in your work. Think like Alice in Wonderland, only this time you are the rabbit. If it surprises you, it will also surprise your customer. People need to want to spend their scant leisure time with you. They need to want to hang out in your store, chill and lounge there. Even some computer stores can pull this off.

It seems the food catering business could learn a lot from these stores...

It's not faith in **TECHNOLOGY**, it's faith in **PEOPLE**

Steve Jobs

Make Sure It Becomes 'App'ealing. It Can Be Done...

Everything starts with the will to do it. For example, doing business in a sustainable, responsible way. Go out and do it, begin today. That is, if you still want to be alive tomorrow. Sustainability comes before everything else. It's not a strategic choice. It's the strategy you need to embrace. It's plan A, because there is no plan B!

Particularly now that Generation Z is starting to take over the jobs, doing business in a non-sustainable way is a no go area. These youngsters won't even consider working for and with you. You'll be butchered in the social media and afterwards you'll be massacred in the real virtual world too. Keeping things in check driven by fear is a thing of the past. Naturally, you can start using modern means, like web care. You can count on one thing, however: online and offline will become one world. This means your reputation is also perceived as a single entity. So just start doing things the green way and you'll be alright.

The younger generation in particular has more than enough confidence. Any problem can be solved. Apple (i.e. ICT) is everyone's best friend and will help everybody get things done with ever fewer operations. All systems will go up in the cloud! In a while, the only place you'll find big, cumbersome computers is a museum. Along with the cassette recorder and the Sony Walkman. Notebooks, netbooks, tablets, and especially smartphones will give anyone access to anything, anywhere. Appmania is definitely and always on the go. Apps exist to make life easier.

Apps will be your guide, your purse, your walking encyclopedia, your GPS, even your conscience. Within five years we'll see the birth of the app that helps you think. By IBM? By Samsung or LG? Or will it be Apple once again, will they manage to make this smart & simple too? Undoubtedly this will be the legacy of Steve Jobs' KISS principle: Keep It Smart and Simple.

Now, let's take a look at your own business or the training you're receiving. What are the consequences for your business model? Have you already started to make things easier for your customers? Be open to these developments and stop putting the brakes on. It's developing in this direction because it's possible. And because it's possible, that's how it will turn out. To quote Fox Mulder from the 'X-files' SF series: "I want to believe."

You can bet your eyes on that...

Let LED Lead the Way

You don't need to be a rocket scientist to add innovative vigor to your products, even your current ones. You just need to be smart and on the lookout for new inventions by others. Because sometimes an innovative idea from a completely different sector can shine a new light on things.

Let's take a look at the new LED lighting technology and its impact on the car industry. Or rather: on the people who are looking to buy a car and base their decision to qualify the car as cool (or not), and buy it (or not), partly on its lighting. Since the introduction of LEDs as daytime running lights, all kinds of cars that are not yet ready for the scrapheap are suddenly being perceived as old-fashioned. An upgrade to a model with LED lighting provides people with a tailor-made alibi for exchanging their old car for a new one, complete with the popular LED strips.

The big sedans built by Porsche, Audi, and BMW were the first to use this technology, but nowadays even the Kias in this world are equipped with the coveted lamps. And the consumers love all of it. So LEDs can make a difference. Then a vacuum cleaner manufacturer thought: "Hey, I can pull off this trick too," and he built a vacuum  cleaner with LED lights. So now you can Hoover in every dark corner. And yes, it sells.

Currently, companies in the US are constructing roads with LEDs incorporated in the tarmac. By day the lights are charged with (sun)light and at night the roads are sufficiently illuminated without the need for street lights or other expensive infrastructural adjustments. So you see, the invention of the LED lamp may act as an accelerator for doing business in a greener, more sustainable, and certainly cooler way.

How could you make use of this LED invention? You won't need to try something 10,000 times, like Edison did; with LED you can make virtually any product hot. Stairs, façades, display windows, coffeemakers, children's toys, and soon the iPad; there is even a pen with a LED. Surely, you won't have to wait very long before you can sleep in a LED bed. A reliable source has sent us a weather report concerning the SENZ storm umbrella: a LED umbrella is imminent. A bright idea, and above all a safe one. Would they be able to generate energy out of rain?

What can you do with such a simple tool?
Use these inventions to your own advantage and make use of innovations that are not originally intended for your line of business. I'm telling you, it will enlighten you.

> Things do not happen.
> Things are MADE TO HAPPEN
>
> John F. Kennedy

pregnancy NOW

Pregnant

If You Don't Provide New Input...

Then everything grinds to a halt. Hence, never let time decide matters for you, always make your own decisions. Some things just happen to you, without you being able to do much about it, that's life. Regard this as a matter of fact, shrug your shoulders and quickly move on. Crying with the wolves for things you can't change anyway is a waste of time. You'll be surprised what you can achieve if you manage to touch and affect people time and time again.

There's no such thing as a free lunch. Lunch may be waiting in three-star restaurants, but you need to go out and pay for it if you want to eat it. The new reality is that you'll always need to take the first step yourself, and even after that you'll still need to push things in the right direction. This means you will need to take the initiative yourself and leave nothing to chance. Others won't do the work for you, you'll only be successful if you go looking for business happiness. Look for the difference you can make, or how you want to be different. Over and over again, you'll need to provide your target group with an alibi to check you out. Marketing will become ever more important. That's why you need to use your marketears & marketeyes more and more!

Plenty of opportunities, but you need to open your ears and eyes. Leave nothing to chance, check Twitter and other social networks and keep track of what's hot, what the trending topics are. Start using web care on these sites, because if you don't check these types of places, you're lost for sure. Not keeping track of SM (social media) can hurt you, just like S & M. By the way, this doesn't mean you need to be active yourself on the social media sites. But the least you can do is follow them, and if you think it's fun, you can join in. But you have to enjoy doing it and turn it into a sport. You can make it happen, even if you're in the service industry, and this way you can attract a lot of attention.

However, if you put your head on the block, you take the risk it'll be chopped off. Always expect some critical comments on your actions. Take George Soros, for instance. He started out as a black market trader, became a financial analyst and created a vast fortune with some pretty smart business deals. He has written eight books about capitalism, finance and society. Although he was convicted and fined for insider trading, he is still well-known for his philanthropic activities. Or take Warren Buffet, they don't come any smarter. His story is one of ongoing success, business wisdom, and of honesty and philanthropy too.

By now, you might be thinking that you're smarter than George or Warren ever were. Great, then why don't you learn how to write and organize a conference for your customers twice a year, and don't forget to invite your hot prospects too. Especially in these hard times, people feel a need for solid investment advice and if you manage to deliver the goods you'll be making a profit again, and growth won't be far away. But stay honest and tell your audience that from now on, 3 to 4% a year is a very decent profit margin. More than 7% will make the public mistrust you and if you mention double-digit percentages, alarm bells will go off.

That's right, the crisis has reinforced everyone's sense of perspective and reality. So get real, engage in realistic marketing. Use your market brain...

Learn and Then Learn Some More and Be Enthusiastic About It!

Every single day, you can learn something from each situation and improve yourself. Although you need to love doing it... Your learning curve stops when you die. Or when you reach the point where you decide not to absorb any more knowledge because you think you know it all; then things automatically come to a halt because you've arrested your own development. And along with it, you've shut yourself off from any (positive) comments that might be very useful to you.

Researchers at Oxford University have discovered that you can become spot on and hot if you succeed in drawing attention to your own learning ability and that of your company. In fact, focusing on learning has proven to be more effective than focusing on achievements. Opening your mind to absorb new information seems to be the most effective way of achieving permanent change. Therefore it's a good idea to read all the books you can possibly find on methods of change. Don't restrict yourself to reading only the biographies of the bold and successful icons, such as Apple front man Steve Jobs or multimedia tycoon Richard Branson. Even though their biographies make good and exciting reading material. Anyhow, if people see you holding a self-help book, they'll think you're a manager who's on the right track. It will be perceived as a sign of strength.

An academic report on learning and reading behavior among managers and business leaders indicated that these DIY books in particular (just like *Great to Cool* and the book you're currently reading!) are read by people who are already actively working on self-guidance. People who've decided long ago that they want to spend time and effort on developing themselves, their company and their private lives. People who are enthusiastic about it. They will achieve a better balance between their private lives and their work, and above all, they'll find more time for their sporting activities. It's undeniable that a healthy mind in a healthy body performs better. But don't be fooled by phrases like 'where there is a will there is a way', or 'swimming upstream makes you stronger'. Of course, you might get stronger doing it, but it's better to let the stream carry you along.

you can also learn a lot from your instincts, such as knowing when to give up the fight. Willpower is a great asset, of course... but it isn't an everlasting power supply. A Dutch mental coach and writer described this process very well: the moment you understand that learning is more important than performing, you'll stand a much better chance of accomplishing what you want. Achieving and performing is often an obsession. On the other hand, learning is a process. Fear can act as a killer and will hold you back. Fear of failure will put the brakes on your personal development. And in general, leaders who're willing to learn are much nicer than overachieving managers. It is definitely important to have a good time with each other. Boorish behavior will be punished and does not encourage others in any way.

From now on, you could decide to learn from all the things you experience and be nicer to others. A smile makes you feel and look a lot better. Your primary affective level will warm up and become hot once you've learned how to laugh again. Under any circumstances.

Listen Sooner and You'll See More ....

If a new employee starts working for your company, don't overload that person's brain with all sorts of rules and regulations right away, and don't try to impose just your own view of the facts. Don't emphasize the way you'd like them to work and perform. No, why don't you do things differently this time? You'll see that you can use the newcomers' views to your best advantage; they're usually more than willing to share their opinions with you. At least, if you act open and supportive while you're getting to know each other. That's exactly the right way to quickly build confidence.

Just point out their desk and tell them how you always did your work. Make sure they understand that you needed to find your way too when you started working. Then give them a week to find out and experience things for themselves. Don't breathe down their necks when they make mistakes, but let them do things their way. Think of the song by Ol' Blue Eyes: *I Did It My Way*.

Invite new employees into your office after their first week and ask them for their views. Ask them what things they would change if it were up to them. You'll hear a lot of things you didn't know yet, but that the new kids on the block see very clearly. Try not to be too defensive. Use their input to start changing things. That'll show them and your customers that your company is modern and up to date. And you'll build genuine confidence between you and the people who work for and with you.

The kids from Generation Z, the latest arrivals in the workplace, will appreciate this cool attitude. They hate hierarchical structures and don't really like being bossed around. But they'll give their life for an inspiring personality who takes the time to listen to them.

How are you going to use their views? After all, they represent the New Global Optimism...

Anna Lindh

From Globalization to Slowbalization!

Large is the new small, fast is becoming the much-loved slow. And cool is hotter than ever. Listen to the trendwatchers and talk to them, debate with them, challenge them. Usually, they're the first ones to see which way certain developments are going. That's because they're looking around and studying their environment all the time, and love to tell others about it and write books or magazine articles on the subject. You can find lots of internationally renowned trendwatchers, like John Naisbitt, Marian Salzman, or Martin Lindstrom.

Although you can also ask the web community about upcoming trends, since the members of Generation Z tend to see things very clearly and at any rate have an opinion on practically everything. These Zs were born between 1992 and the present and can safely be regarded as digital natives, as completely opposed to the older generation of digital dummies. Round about 2020 they will start to take control of business life. Together with psychologist and marketing strategist Jos Ahlers we've researched this generation, for example by using the Whatsapp method in this somewhat crazy study. Our motto: "It's better to be more or less right than to be completely wrong." Of course we've also considered the (on & offline) sellers and recent and future developments in our study.

One of the things the Z-youngsters love is the slow food and regional products movement. Small village shops that sell their homegrown produce, or buy vegetables and meat from local farmers. This way, no valuable resources are wasted in ferrying foodstuffs all around the country or between countries. Globalization has turned into Slowbalization. The things you can get from your own region taste better, they are greener and give you a warm feeling, because you are helping your own neighbors to make a living.

This is just what Generation Z expects from offline stores: a sense of togetherness and inspiration. The local grocery store provides this on a local scale, but large international chain stores will try to accomplish this by establishing ever larger and more spectacular flagship stores, such as the Australian Ugg Flagship Store in New York. These retailers will mainly use their stores to spread their brand's message. Social cohesion on the one hand, and theatrical showmanship on the other. Nevertheless, both extremes have two things in common: emotion and inspiration. The days of using a store as a rational distribution centre are almost over. This is a sure thing, especially since many clothes stores manage to look like the average charity shop. If it's just about buying things, Generation Z will do this online with a few simple mouse clicks, just like other consumers. They'll have the stuff brought to them.

Because online, you can compare quality and prices, find the cheapest products and find out what your friends think of the purchases you have planned. Moreover... web shops can ignore shopping hours; they're open 24/7.

All this implies that the new consumer will shop in two different ways: online, in an effective, efficient and cheap way through the clicks; and offline, at the mall, where they'll go for emotional, relaxing and inspired, through the bricks. In cases where efficient shopping is combined with an inspired online environment, traditional retail stores are very right to view this as a real threat. Currently there are quite a few examples of web shops that link the advantages of doing your shopping online to a strong emotional message. It's much harder to do this offline. For example: the online T-shirt store Threadless.com. Customers can send in their T-shirt designs, other customers can comment on these designs, and in the end the web store will actually use the best designs to produce T-shirts. So far, they've already received about 375,000 designs. This way, Threadless is not only efficient, but extremely inspiring.

To top this, offline retailers (i.e. the regular stores) will really need to offer more than a nice assortment, good prices and a pleasant store. Otherwise they won't get many visits from Generation Z. The offline store needs to become part of the regular network of the young Generation Z. Retailers will need to involve them, share the store's experience with them, get to know them personally and offer inspiration. Make your shop more theatrical, offline as well as online. The free cup of coffee at the espresso bar at the back of the store is a nice starting point, but nothing more. It's more important to employ staff that make a difference. It's all about the shift from companies based on IQ to EQ-driven business...

How do you beguile your potential customers? Yes, desire is the keyword. In 3 seconds you can feel it: hey, it's nice in here... let's take it slow, let's not leave in a hurry!

> Chaos often breeds **LIFE** when order breeds **HABIT**
>
> — Henry Adams

Chaos Equals Opportunity: The Chinese Use the Same Symbol for Both Concepts...

Well how's that, opportunity is written in the same way as chaos in Chinese? How wise and how astute, because opportunities are often accompanied by chaotic circumstances. That's because a number of things in this world need to change fundamentally and that will always make people feel uneasy. The right decisions need to be taken, not in a shortsighted manner, but resolutely and above all, adequately.

Coach and motivator Tony Robbins once said: "It is in your moments of decision that your destiny is shaped." That's real wisdom for you, which we all acknowledge and which urges us to make the right decisions. But do you actually put it into practice? You'll need to start listening more to your intuitive, inner voice. You know: the voice that talks to you all the time. With men, the voice sits somewhere in their abdomen and never stops talking. With women, the voice is in their head and it starts working by the time they go to bed. That's when women tend to rationalize the emotions they have experienced during the daytime, and start planning ahead for the next day.

Your intuitive voice gives you advice based on 'reason coupled with rush'. So why don't we listen to it every single time? The problem is that such a decisive moment is very hard to define! Usually you can only tell afterwards whether you've made the right decision at such a point. And it can make all the difference. Anyway, decisive moments often have something to do with meeting someone.

My encounter with Richard Branson was such a moment; it has truly brought me a lot of good things. I really wish everyone could experience a kind of 'Branson moment'. When you talk with someone like him you can feel that there's more between heaven and earth, you can feel his knowledge flow into you, as it were. And I had the same feeling when I met Dutch management guru Eckhart Wintzen. That goes to show you, during our lifetime every one of us will encounter some people who prove to be important to us, and with these encounters several opportunities will present themselves to us too. But not everybody will grab these opportunities and many of us have no idea why. Fear of the unknown? The chaos it might induce? What is it that decides whether we really open ourselves up to opportunities and start to act upon them?

Here's a surprise for you: you are the one who decides and nobody else. Since we are going through the umpteenth crisis, this might be the right time to break through the code. Try to find exactly those people who can make the difference for you. Re-read the book that used to excite you and stimulate you and made you teem with energy.

We shape our future at a few decisive points in time, by meeting people that prove to be crucial for us. You need to realize that you make the difference. Just listen to the late Robert Palmer's *She Makes My Day* (and the difference too) and you'll never forget it. So kick off the trend and start changing. If you just keep following others, you'll often step into the muck of the herd, this is a crude saying but oh so true. Start living your life more energetically and create some chaos for yourself for a change. The opportunities you create in this way could be the best ones you've had in years!

We Need Bridge-Builders...

The most frequently asked question is: how do I become as successful as I was when times were better? Well, this will happen if your customers truly want you to get the order, assignment, or deal. If they feel good granting you things. The more desire you can put into your company's DNA, the better your chances are for the future. Unfortunately, past success offers no guarantee for the future. Fear and legal measures aren't very stimulating factors for growth, nor for holding on to what you've got for that matter.

Nowadays, any little disagreement is enough to start hiring lawyers and go to court. Not just in case of a divorce, but also between companies and between a company and the local or federal government. That's because the authorities want to play an ever-increasing role in business life. On the other hand, employing a mediator in order to prevent the case from going to court has become 'hot' too. In itself this is a good idea, but at the same time it's also a sign of weakness; you clearly demonstrate that you're not able to solve your problems as grown-ups.

The biggest problem often lies in the egos of the people involved and in the inability to acknowledge each other's strengths. Nearly all conflicts arise from attacks of blind rage, which prevent people from acting rationally and solving their problems. We've forgotten how to hold back and count to 20 before responding. Despite the fact that we've entered the era of the 'sheconomy' – where women are clearly very influential in business matters – oddly enough, many men and women have adopted a kind of macho behavior. This type of behavior needs to be stopped, because it will prevent us from making fundamental changes and it'll stand in the way of your company's growth.

Actually, what you need is not a mediator but a viewpoint; stop fighting immediately, let everybody know you're done with your battles and make it clear that you'd like to reach an agreement.

Relinquishing the fight and letting go of your aggressive thoughts will allow you to breathe freely again, and may shine a completely different light on any disagreements. Try to come to a true reconciliation and an understanding. You never know. As soon as you stop fighting you'll see the positive energy flow back into your company and the market. You'll be able to fully focus your attention again without needing to listen to the militant voice in your head, the aggressive voice that holds you back.

you are the only person who can build such a bridge, you will only benefit from this. You'll see: lots of people will wish you well and grant you their business.

> I figure lots of PREDICTIONS is best. People will forget the ones I get wrong and MARVEL OVER THE REST

Alan Cox

Become Technotolerant Too...

Let's stop thinking in terms of 'this can't possibly become true.' Especially now. You have to believe anything's possible, since the predictions in technology are so positive! Often these predictions are so miraculous that you tend to frown a bit and in the back of your head hear a skeptical murmur: 'surely this can't be true, I don't believe it.' Mute that internal voice for a second. Skip reading the papers for a day and think of what wonderful things can be achieved if we allow them to happen, if we allow the future to happen.

We won't have a lot of choice; if we keep behaving like electrical power junkies, fossil fuels will run out even sooner than expected. Big Blue, a.k.a. the huge electronics company IBM, recently predicted that the energy you yourself generate could very well become the fastest growing energy source in future. Why shouldn't it be possible to transform human motion into useful energy? Each and every moving item can produce energy, think of the water running through the sewers, for example. But you can also derive energy from your shoes, and even daylight can act as a power source while you travel from A to B. In future we'll store all this energy in a small device that we carry along all the time, which collects energy. And let's not forget the development of the energy tree, a synthetic tree, plant or shrub, produced in an environmentally friendly way, using nanotechnology, that is able to transform light, heat and movement into 100% green and sustainable electricity. Why don't you Google it and see for yourself!

Others predict that we'll eventually be freed of passwords and PIN codes, once biometric checks have become commonplace. In about five years' time, the sound of your voice, a fingerprint or an iris scan could be enough to safely get your money from an ATM machine. Using this technique, it could also become possible to access the iCloud and take a look at your own patient file. Of course, in such situations you would need to guarantee everyone's privacy, so better safety measures will be sorely needed. If we don't take care, the pirates will take over, here and everywhere else. Internet crime is relatively new, but we're all going to have to deal with it. Current Phishing activities are nothing compared to the invasion of your private life once your BlackBerry or notebook has been hacked. Technology stops at nothing these days. What about the following example? By now, we're quite capable of measuring and analyzing the electrical currents within the brain. The Hollywood movie *What Women Want*, about reading women's minds and using this knowledge to score points in the field of marketing, will become a reality. Well, almost. Is this a daydream or will it become a nightmare, such as shown in *The X-files* or *The Shining*?

Mark my words: it's going to turn out the way you want, provided you start acting upon it. We haven't come so far that we're able to transfer our thoughts to our BlackBerry and let the machine dial the people we're thinking of, but smart scientists are already trying to link the human brain to various devices such as computers or smartphones. Do you want to call someone? Just think about this person. Don't forget, this would be a great invention for people who are paralyzed, but can still use their brain. The human robot is starting to come into the picture, a wonderful solution for those who are in rehab after an accident or illness. Because of the developments in the field of Artificial Intelligence and neurology we'll perhaps come to understand what autistic people experience. Imagine having your private doctor in your pocket all the time.

In this respect, the finest prediction is the notion that in two or three years time there won't be any spam anymore. Wow, that would be great! No longer any Viagra e-mails, no shady letters from Nigeria begging for money and no fake inheritance from a long-forgotten great-aunt. This will all be over. It will become possible to attune messages to the (often mobile) recipient to such an extent that all messages received will only be relevant and not even perceived as spam. Also, all twitterers will adhere to a new 'twittiquette' which will be self-regulating. This will put a stop to the darker aspects of this beautiful new medium. Crude and one-sided shouting matches will be a thing of the past.

Now all we need to do is behave in an adult way and only use these new technologies to solve the problems that matter. How tolerant will you become in the near future? Let these developments take their course and you'll see: good things will happen. And those few mistakes? They can easily be overshadowed by all the great initiatives you deploy, time after time... in order to win!

Who Cares Where You Buy It, and When...

What does it matter where you buy or sell something and when? When will some of the (religious) politicians finally acknowledge that citizens can make up their own minds how and when to live and buy? And that more rules will only widen the gap between the government and its citizens? Because this will undoubtedly turn into a long period of suffering for all parties involved, even with respect to their own fan base! Naturally, those who wish to regard the seventh day as a day of rest can quietly stay at home and go to church, just as they please. Those who celebrate the Sabbath are free to keep on doing this. Do you want to go to the mosque every day? No problem. Please, let everybody be the judge of their own spare time, let people do what they want, when they want. These mechanisms will surely become self-regulating.

In the Bible belt, few shopkeepers would dare to open their shops on a Sunday. But where fertile economic grounds can be found, a plentiful retail community will bloom. And that is a good thing, because wherever people can move and buy, a new mini-economy will arise. This kind of economy will be boosted by things like a health food stand in the street, where you can see how fresh food is prepared with love and attention. In that respect we're taking our cue from Asia more and more; the accompanying smile works wonders.

In time we'll no longer eat three meals a day, but we will slowly grow towards seven food breaks. Particularly the food sector will profit from a new local shopping and buying spree. But keep in mind that for the first time, you can detect some small cracks in the consumers' 24/7 buying behavior. Especially the youngsters from Generation Z enjoy shopping in the city, provided the prices are reasonable compared to online. You also see people from Generations X and Y, and even baby boomers, shop around on the net but subsequently decide to purchase the goods 'live'; as long as the store is open when they need it to be open.

Here's a tip for those who own shops in areas where they still have restrictions on Sunday shopping. Just open your web store 24/7, or use an Appvertising QR code (a kind of bar code) which can be scanned from your shop window. Give people who use this code a 5% discount and you'll be surprised at how many people are prepared to use this offer. Yours truly tried out this method in a Dutch town with strict Sunday shopping rules, together with a market researcher. The turnover for that month increased by 6%. Coincidence or just plain smart?

What can you do to satisfy your customer's buying interest 24/7? The technology is already there, since governmental techno-(in)tolerance can never stop these developments.

So...

Hope Alone Is Not Enough...

From now on, leave nothing to chance and make sure that you use all possible means to hype your product or service, but your show or musical too. Just hoping for success is not enough; you really need to invest some energy if you want to create a hype. Just like the record companies in the old days, you need to start plugging your merchandise. I discovered this myself when I started to market *Great to Cool* and *Generation Z*. Laying on a prayer mat with your head towards Mecca is no use, nor is lighting candles in front of a statue of the Blessed Virgin Mary, because nothing will happen. You need to push forward and use your common sense. Fortunately it's great fun! And oh-so-cool to do.

In the States it's a well-known fact: "He who has health has hope; and he who has hope has everything." But in present times hope alone is not enough. You need to strive for more and pull out all the stops to lend wings to the success you'd so dearly like to have. You will need to create this passion and enthusiasm personally. Just providing the product or producing the musical doesn't automatically make it successful. Nowadays it's all about promotion and campaigning. Of course it all starts with a top-of-the-line product. Due to the enormous supply available these days, this is the very first requirement. And then... the game commences. Start playing with all the different variables you can find that might lead to the '3" wow'. And remember, always use the curiosity factor of the people in your target group.

Isn't it beautiful to watch people come to the preview of the new BMW 6, months before the car has even arrived in the car dealers' showrooms? Or surf the Internet in search of the new Porsche convertible? "Be the first to know," CNN's long-time slogan, is a primal urge that lives in all of us. To be the front-runner, the first to know the news and have the scoop. Just see how Dutch show producer John de Mol goes about it. First he sells his TV format to lots of other countries, including the US, where it is known as *The Voice*. Then he manages to keep the public's attention focused on his show by periodically changing members of the jury, or the show's presenter. Once again, the goal is accomplished: people are talking about his show.

A hype is something you create yourself. Now don't think: "I've just got a small shop, my name is not John de Mol." You have the same opportunities as they have and if you use the social media, it won't cost you a dime... People love to notice you've got something new to offer, especially if you tell them they're the first to be told in person. You'll be giving them an alibi to come and visit you again.

If you don't take action, there's always a chance people will drop by unexpectedly of course. But if you stay good friends with hope & hype, at least you won't have left anything to chance. And if someone happens to enter your shop by sheer coincidence, then that's an added bonus.

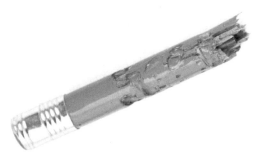

Take the Stress Test, It'll Make You Feel Better!

Nobody had ever thought it possible, but it happened anyway. First, the bankruptcy of companies that were deemed 'too big to fail': the Enron energy company and financial services firm Lehman Brothers. By now even entire countries are threatened with bankruptcy, the euro is in trouble and the world economy has stopped growing. Wow, what an opportunity to re-examine and review everything! It's a good idea not to wait until it's too late. Although this is the year of the Dragon, it doesn't mean that our misery has to drag on.

Why don't you do the same as the banks are currently forced to do under pressure from the International Monetary Fund or some other authority? Think of events that nobody ever thought possible, things that were never on the official agenda! Until recently, the worst-case scenarios of several airline companies had never included a volcanic ash cloud that would severely inhibit air traffic. But now they know better. By the way, these events can teach you a lot about using social media to stay in touch with everyone! Nowadays anything goes…

Take nuclear power, for example; this form of energy seemed on the rise again. After all, Chernobyl was 25 years ago. But then the Japanese tsunami struck and the Fukushima plant exploded. Just imagine what it'd be like to lose 20% of your customers in a single day! What would you do to keep things going? What would you do to maintain control and how long could you hold out until better times? Try to imagine it, and then do the same thing for a 40% decline in customers; try to calculate how long your reserves would last to keep you in business. Let's say you're in the fashion business and the country where you buy your goods suddenly goes bankrupt. Where would you buy your stock? This is not a fantasy. It could happen any day.

But there are many more examples of getting out of the frying pan and into the (dragon's) fire. For instance, if you own a beauty parlor and the brand of products you've used for years appears to be a lot less animal-friendly than you always thought. Bye bye turnover, so long customers... And what about the news on leaking and unsafe breast implants? Those lovely C cups will all need to be replaced by plastic surgeons, but who's going to pay for it? Ask yourself these kinds of questions more often and make sure you have some kind of liability insurance. You'll feel safer. Businesswise, it's never a good idea to put all your eggs in one basket. It's better to adopt a "pony-and-horse" strategy. If your horse has difficulty walking for a while, just mount your pony, pull up your legs a bit and trot on.

Now don't go thinking this won't happen to you. Believe me, we'll all suffer the consequences of the economic slowdown. But those who are first to discover the need to stretch the envelope will not only survive these times, they may even grow thanks to the crisis. How will you react to the stress test, when things you never thought possible start happening to you?

If You're Stuck, Turn to TED!

The net is full of inspiration, but you need to know where to look. For example, take a good look at TED. "Ideas worth spreading" is the great idea underlying this movement and their website. And yes, it gets things moving all right...

It's unbelievably fascinating to see how the real entrepreneurs have chosen their words, brimming with wisdom, and how they manage to captivate and bind the critical TED audience. The words of marketing consultant Simon Sinek must have been quoted innumerable times, all over the word, amazing! Look up his name on the web and let Simon explain to you how easy it actually is to be successful. With a magic marker and a flip over-chart he'll patiently explain that everything revolves around: WHY, HOW, and WHAT! In fact, would that be Apple's secret too?

Imagine that your presentation is the last you'll ever give: then take a look at Randy Pausch' website, the information technology specialist who passed away in 2008. That will give you pause for thought and you'll immediately realize what the essence of life is. Listen to a ten-year-old boy explaining that the kids from Generation Z know a lot more about current and future technology, and how to build an app that's so hot that everyone wants to have it: a bit like teenage heartthrob Justin Bieber, but not quite the same...

TED will give you ideas that are worthwhile, ideas you should discuss with your management team. But it's also a source of some hilarious presentations that will make you laugh your head off when you watch them on your iPad. Meanwhile, you'll find hundreds of people on TED who would surely help you if you needed some advice. TED generates energy and if you pass on this energy and inject it into your own company, to improve the mood and give some guidance, you'll be doing exactly what TED proposes to do: spread the message!

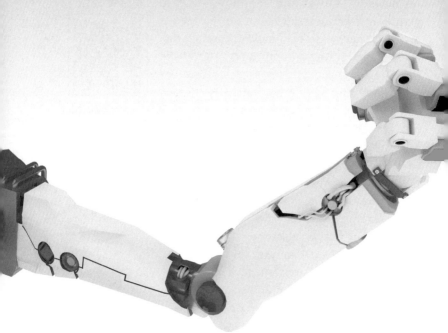

Change Your Business Model and Your Outlook Will Improve

A lot of time is wasted on silly discussions that arise from a defensive attitude, which is usually only directed at maintaining the status quo. But why would you postpone adapting your business model until it's virtually inevitable? It is undoubtedly a good thing to react to changing markets, but anticipating these changes is even better, as the example below demonstrates.

When they were inventing the Nespresso concept, Nestlé company marketeers wondered what would happen if you eliminated the distribution of coffee by wholesalers and supermarkets, which at the time was the decisive success factor! After all, 98% of all coffee was sold and bought in such stores, and companies that wanted to excel in coffee were facing a hell of a job. Their train of thought went like this: given these figures, it would be much easier to excel in the sector where the other 2% is sold, since the competition would be much less fierce there! Finally, after years of hard work and trying, they've managed it. Yet it wasn't easy to determine this new strategy. Or was it? Imagine that the most important, decisive factor in your company's success would change or vanish overnight, and think of ways to react to this. This is not just a playful exercise, it often hands you the key to future success. Why don't you Google Patrick van der Pijl and experience how you can visualize your strategies?

You don't need to invest a whole lot, all you need to do is read Alexander Osterwalder's *Business Model Generation*. This wonderful book, written in a clear and comprehensible style, is aimed at analyzing and questioning older, outdated business models and at challenging them to change. Anyone can turn around imaginative and visionary ideas within the playing field of changing business models, ideas that challenge established concepts, enliven them or even rejuvenate them. This book tells you everything you should know, quickly, in a simple way and with attractive visual elements. Examples are presented by using illustrations, and as we know, an image says more than 10,000 words in this era of visual information. The Business Model Canvas is a great tool for describing, analyzing and designing business models and it's based on the concepts of leading business thinkers. You know, helping to develop innovative business models is very stimulating and energizing. On top of this, you'll get five free business model themes for future reference. After all, some institution may suddenly make a decision that leaves you with your back against the wall; then you'll have to rethink your strategies.

Here's a practical example: at a summer summit, the cream of the crop from an international brewery's staff were confronted with the hypothetical situation that President Obama was going to sign legislation to ban the production of beer containing alcohol, at the request of the international Islamic community. What were their options? Of course, they could deny this reality, even if it was fictional, or they could stir up the best brains in the organization and let them come up with new ways to cope with the changing rules of the game. And do it within 72 hours. And that's what they did. During their quest they discovered something that might cause the SOS of beer, the Share Of Stomach, to grow by 10% worldwide. We're definitely going to hear more about this tasty, non-alcoholic beer. This kind of beer is also suitable for Friday afternoon meetings, since these meetings are going to replace the weekly Monday morning briefing. Only, please don't call this new beer brand 'Buckler', because that name was permanently ruined when Dutch comedian Youp van 't Hek satirized Buckler's image in his shows.

What about you? Are you going to anticipate the future in the same way? It may give you more innovative power, and a head start that is not yet visible to your competitor for the time being...

> The great problem of the concert hall is that the shoebox is the ideal shape for acoustics but that **NO ARCHITECT** worth their **NAME** wants to build a shoebox

Rem Koolhaas

Look It Up... and Inhale Inspiration!

No, this isn't about your e-mail or your What's app, although looking things up is a good idea, because the number of (spelling) mistakes has grown explosively since the iPad has arrived. It's about the Library of Congress! You can go name hunting there, for free. It's a wonderful thing in itself to be able to search through authentic manuscripts and events and research the actual facts of the past. Like the diary of Thomas Jefferson, for example. But you may also find some painful memories, like documents on the battles of the Civil War, or voices from the days of slavery.

From a business point of view, it might be smarter to go looking for glorious names from the past. You don't really need to reinvent the wheel. Some of the world's famous brand names have simply been found in the telephone directory: TOD's for example, the shoe brand (nowadays it's also a clothing brand), named after a private citizen discovered in the Boston, MA telephone directory. If you're looking for a name for your new strategy or brand, the Library of Congress is particularly rich hunting ground. You can rediscover all kinds of details on nearly forgotten names. Such as the Pullman Palace Car Company, which manufactured railroad cars in the mid-to-late 19th century, or the Tucker Torpedo, a very advanced automobile produced in Detroit in 1948. And you can find lots of other imaginative names and brands. For that matter, a visit to the Clinton Foundation in Little Rock, AR, will provide you with lots of inspiration too.

You see, names are important for the DNA of your product, since the Top of Brand Awareness is able to explain what the product's about in mere seconds and will make sure that the brand pops up in the customer's mind automatically. You might also try another strategy, namely choosing a name that so closely resembles the name of your (successful) competitor's brand that the competitor wants to sue you. That'll make you world-famous in a minute! Of course, Apple and Orange produce different things, but the basic idea behind the name is the same. But Pepsi-Cola is very similar to Coca Cola, and the products are very similar too. This led to the 'Cola-wars' of the 1980s, set off by the Pepsi Challenge, where blindfolded consumers compared Pepsi to Coca Cola.

If your product is very similar to your competitor's product, you will also become a candidate for a takeover bid from the other company. Just take a look at the development of various brand names, then you'll see how this works. You will be surprised at the comments people make if the name is so obvious that they think it's child's play to come up with such a name. Don't be mistaken: such a name is worth its weight in gold. So put up a fight if you want to hang on to the name you have chosen, especially if you're convinced this name is going to attract lots of customers.

Make sure you find a catchy name, one that allows you to claim the status of 'the Original' right away, even as a startup company. A name that enables you to create the bubble that will float your startup and that secures you the right domain name in the cloud, in such a way that even Apple comes knocking on your door because you're coming too close for comfort. And because they can't take any legal measures to stop you. Then the only thing they can do is make a takeover bid, as one Israeli company experienced recently. But it can happen to you too.

What's your next range, service, or product going to be called? Or are you brave enough to reinvent the shoebox and simply call it a shoebox? When you're stuck, ask the crowd, or go name surfing at the Library of Congress.

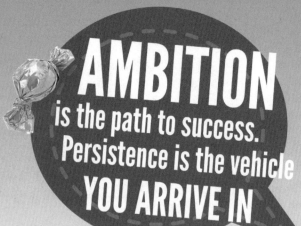

Stop That Passion Nonsense!

Don't take me wrong, it is very clear what you mean by 'passion'. The problem is, everywhere I go, all over the globe, 'passion' is one of the keywords in the CEO's speech and often mentioned as a core value. Entire books are written on the concept, often good books, ones worth reading. To be passionate about something is perceived as a good thing, which it is, but nowadays the term is so easily misinterpreted that it can fool a lot of people. Some examples: "Your Potential. Our Passion," or "Passion to advance our clients, passion to realize our ideas." What does it mean? A famous Dutch clown called 'Bassie' (also pronounced as Passie, which means passion in Dutch) had the public fooled with a crazy TV commercial, and in fact, that's what the word passion does.

The funny thing is that the word passion is used so often, whether appropriately or not, that it is starting to lose its meaning and value. My advice is to use a synonym if you want to get the message across. The term 'ambition' is often more to the point, for example. It points us in a certain direction and it conveys energy. And it doesn't have any vague connotations; it's one of the healthiest characteristics of a company or employee. You see, you can truly distinguish yourself by your energetic ambition, if you manage to convey it or have your website convey the message. It's perfectly clear and a good incentive for people to want to know more about your company.

Why don't you take a close look at your mission statement or the personnel forms used by your Human Resources department or even your job offers: do they contain the word 'passion'? Maybe even your pay-off line uses the word? For example: "Food is our passion," "A passion for service," or "It is my passion to help you!" There are hundreds of examples on the web, but do they distinguish themselves? Does it provide the 3" hook, does it attract attention within 3 seconds? Cross out that word and replace it by ambition! Passion has become a word that is overused and barely understood.

Listen carefully, what does your conscience say? "Yes, he's right," or "What bullshit, I really am the passionate entrepreneur whom everyone should get to know." If the latter is really the case, then you're good... If not, you know what to do!

The Brands & Tastes of Days Gone by, the Technology of the Future...

Each crisis also has its advantages: if you stand still for a minute you can reflect on what you're doing. You'll be forced to think more deeply on how to go ahead. And once the good times return, you'll be in the winning orbit. That's enough reason for KLM and Virgin to continue developing commercial space travel.

A worldwide analysis shows that during the present crisis, people are getting nostalgic about the past, they're longing for the old days. This doesn't mean they wish to go back to those times, because in most cases they were far less prosperous than now. Imagine you were set back to the situation you were in three or four years ago. Did you really have it so bad, here in the Western world? Of course not, you were better off than the previous year, but the problem is you get used to it so quickly. Even if you're looking for a new job at the moment, try to work out what you actually need to make a decent living. Don't work on the basis of the top salary you were earning before you were fired, because your salary depends heavily on the economic climate, just like the stock exchange. Past earnings and profits provide no guarantee for the future, so it's far from certain that you'll be able to earn your former salary in future.

It's the same with our nostalgia for old-fashioned brands. Until recently, this trend was called 'retro'. Now it has become HOTro. Very trendy and brought to you once again, intended to let you dream away, by your nostalgia-based EQ. In your perception, the bread of days past was much tastier than today's bread. As a result, old-fashioned bread returns, produced with traditional methods and locally grown wheat. In the same way, heirloom vegetables will become more popular again. Our taste buds will have a party in our mouths and we'll start to use less salt in our food anyway. The Dutch Maaslander cheese company will really applaud this trend, since they've been producing low-salt cheese for several years and claim that this makes you taste the cheese better, which is true. But small and simple brands that dare to be authentic will quickly become more popular, since they're more than cool. The FLIP camera is good proof of this. As is the new John Phone. Nothing to do with a smartphone, just a cell phone you can use for phone calls. Nothing more and nothing less.

In this respect, the Fiat 500 is completely based on the principle of HOTro. BMW's Mini takes it even a step further and pushes the boundaries within this type of cars. Top design & technology in a package that seems to be completely up-to-date, but is firmly rooted in the nostalgic memory, nevertheless. Nike just experienced the same thing; people have literally battled to get their hands on Nike's replica Air Jordans. And we're not just talking sleeping bags in front of stores, but regretfully some real fights too, as well as burglaries at the homes of the lucky individuals who managed to buy a pair. All that for a pair of sneakers. Watch it on YouTube. You won't believe your eyes.

Or will you? Dream on a bit, which flavor could you bring back from the past with your company? Which seemingly lost service could you reintroduce? Do it! Before you know it, you'll have secured a place in the consumer's memory. The HOT throw (HOTro) in the mind. Yes, HOT will quickly be rooted in the brain, provided you manage to insert it in the right way (3"). Because the path to success starts in the brain. There you produce a substance that's unbeatable. You'll no longer need to sell; you will be bought instead.

Put That Tie Back On!

What's hip and what's lame? What are the absolute dos and don'ts? What's hot and what's not? In other words: how do you manage to stay at the top of the charts of what is hip, cool and hot? There is no recipe, it just happens. However, you actually can influence some of these charts right before they're drafted. Have you ever wondered where all these lists come from and who compiles them? Some compilers even have the nerve to claim that their chart is the one and only ranking!

As a rule, these lists are mostly made up by the best trendwatchers on the planet. Those who dare to extrapolate data to future developments purely on the basis of observation and experience, without benefiting from these predictions in a commercial, political, or ideological sense. True and genuine, so to speak. Some journalists try their hand at predicting the future too, once in a while. Investigative journalists are often a lot like trendwatchers in that they write great stories but they tend to find themselves in trouble when they need to climb the stage and present them. You see, speaking in public is a real skill, especially if you try to radiate enthusiasm and drive and try to take the audience along on your trip through the future. It's the same as writing: lots of top editors are capable of writing their columns in such a way that you read them until the last letter and are amazed at their lists of what's hip or uncool. So much so that your inner voice – there it is again – is surprised too: "Oh, really? No, that can't be right."

For instance: aging gracefully is totally cool nowadays; the same goes for introducing quality into your life. Quantity is over. A few wrinkles, no problem at all, but preferably from laughing a lot! Radio is making a worldwide comeback, as opposed to all sorts of visual media. Just like vulnerable leadership with a clear, comprehensible mission, a mission you can support. You will also see the return of good manners; saying 'sir' is becoming cool again. And vapidly twittering into space is so very uncool. Actually, the new Twitter etiquette might cause you to be banned to the outfield of the Twitter net if you don't watch your language. Dutch historian Maarten van Rossem, specialized in American affairs, speaks of "fact-free politics," in which every politician is allowed to issue statements without being held to the truth or checked; well, hopefully these tendencies will soon be outdated. A thing of the past, preferably. This kind of politics will no longer be taken seriously, but will be condemned because of its lack of serious content.

Once you have landed in the Twitter cemetery by such silly actions, the way back out is very, very hard. Unless you deeply bow your head and offer your sincere apologies. Since we happen to be talking about things that are hip, why don't we stir up things some more: the (neck)tie is coming back into fashion. Yes, that's right, the tie is fashionable again, and will be more stylish than ever. A pity for the late Dutch Prince Claus, who once addressed a meeting of bankers and ostentatiously removed his necktie as a sign of newfound freedom. This gesture has inspired lots of people and encouraged me to not wear a tie for years. But due to the crisis, the tie is making a comeback. Currently, anything that's cool has a lot to do with security, with avoiding risks. The fashionable and hip brands exude a feeling of safety, of being grounded, going back to their roots.

Is your brand among these too? Reflect on this and remember, everything that's hot needs to be continually maintained and needs to conquer its place on the 'green' chart. By the way, green is the new cool color, for the next 50 years! Not as a fashionable color, but as a basic attitude for everything we do. So make sure you do it well, otherwise the public will strangle you with your own tie...

BEND, break or kill the rules says GAGA! She's from NYC! So, break down barriers and **IGNORE LIMITS**

René C.W. Boender

Get Clever, Negotiate Your Rent!

Of course it's **ridiculous that rents can be raised without** any clear motive. It is about time that the landlords of today open their eyes to the new reality, because currently everyone is economizing and turnovers and profits are under pressure. Negotiations have never been so prevalent and quite a few prices are now based on fair profit share. Whether you rent office space or a store, in a top location or not, the new rules of the game have become harsher than ever. Everyone's bargaining…

Even in fashion stores, people ask for a discount and get 10% off without too much trouble. The same goes for the electronics store. Will fixed prices become a thing of the past and will all consumers become so empowered? If that's the case, you can surely negotiate the rent you're currently paying. Take the first step yourself and start playing this game of chess with the white pawn. That way you'll always be a step ahead. You could get 'No' for an answer, but maybe there is a 'Yes' in store for you, somewhere in the future. Your landlord may want to hang on to the present lease, but there's always a chance he's willing to listen to you. It's clear that landlords have common sense too. Company directors who lease their premises to their own company, also lower the rent when they see they can no longer cough up the money. Naturally, some landlords will hide their head in the sand and pretend there's nothing wrong. But beware, chances are that they'll get stuck with empty premises, and these chances are increasing by the day, with all sorts of bad consequences.

Even the faithful tenant that has suffered your conditions for 15 years will start wondering if it isn't time for a change. And soothing talk won't help. Smart landlords, who want to stay friends with their tenants and keep doing business, will change tack. These times require greater flexibility, which means that the rents will no longer be indexed as a matter of course, but will increasingly become related to business profits and turnovers.

If you make more than you expected, the landlord will profit from this too. This could mean that the rent is split up in a fixed and a variable part; a low basic rent and a variable part which depends on the business's turnover. This is already happening

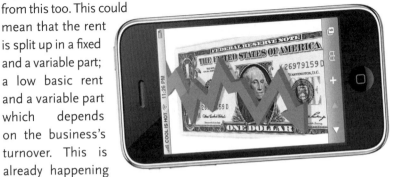

in parts of the US, to prevent shops and offices from remaining unoccupied for long periods of time. And it also serves to introduce a new business model in this line of business, in which the traditional, automatic way of indexing was set in stone.

So why isn't this model adopted everywhere? You can definitely see cracks appearing in the brickwork. Even if the rent is not your direct responsibility, why don't you bring this subject up in the next meeting, now you've read this chapter? Who knows, maybe your initiative will enliven your business model and give your company some breathing space so it can survive these hard times. The rules are meant to be bent a little, aren't they? If the landlord refuses to budge, you can always give notice and you'll be surprised at the consequences.

Music Does Much More Than Enhance the Mood...

You only need to hear a single note and you remember the lyrics, even if you haven't heard that particular song in years. Music does something to your mood. Guitar legend Jimi Hendrix once said: "Music doesn't lie. If there is something to be changed in this world, then it can only happen through music."

Protest songs often act as a catalyst for change in the world, but of course music can accomplish much more, also with regard to consumers' buying attitude. In Belgium they recently tested this attitude towards music by installing similar music systems in two delicatessens. They wanted to find out whether music can arouse consumer interest as well as enhance people's moods. A bit like how smells work: you know, in the doorway you smell the aroma of freshly baked bread and you suddenly get a craving for bread. Back to the music test. One of the shops started playing a popular Belgian radio station with soft pop music, the other shop played traditional French chansons and classical music. Before both shops were equipped with this superb HiFi system, they both attracted about the same number of customers with the same average spending pattern. After a month, both shops had increased their turnover. The shop that played pop music saw its turnover increase by 3.8%, while the number of customers stayed the same. The shop that played the French chansons and classical music increased its turnover by 6.8%. After three months these percentages became even higher and so did the 'Customer Satisfaction Index' numbers for both businesses. Previously, the average Customer Satisfaction Index was 7.8 for both shops. After three months this had become significantly higher; the pop music store scored an 8.1 and the classical music store an 8.4. Also, the average amount spent by customers had gone up, especially when the music was also softly audible outside the shops (at about 10% of the original volume). From the outside you could already hear and sample the mood inside, and most customers concluded the food would be great in such a shop!

In the US, the Panera Bread bakery chain swears by classical music too, just pay them a visit and you will start enjoying yourself while you are waiting for your order. It mellows you out and you'll start to look at the world more mildly.

But music can also stimulate you, especially during a sale. During the crazy summer sales, a good beat is recommended. That gives you energy. It works the same way in the car dealer's showroom and in the office. Music provides a great background and even makes you do your work better. Although not every manager is convinced. Only, don't just tune in to some radio station without thinking, but reflect on the reasons for looking up this station.

KIIS? WPLJ-FM? Or rather the classic rock on KLOS-FM? If you're in the retail business, make sure to play some well-known pop music in the mornings. In the afternoons a middle-of-the-road music blend will do. It doesn't really matter what you play, as long as it enhances the mood and gets people in the buying mood. Although you might need to be a bit careful with late night music or jazz; you don't want your customers to get drowsy or fall asleep while shopping, do you? And if you own a cheese shop, you will see that the sale of your French cheese products will soar if you play some quiet French music in your store. Don't hesitate, just turn on the music.

With the new wireless iPod Bose system, these things are within everybody's (price) range. Your customers will reward you with larger turnovers. And the world will become a nicer place to be. That's what music can accomplish...

Learn from the 'Attention Captivators'. And Absorb Their Wisdom...

How do you attract attention, and how do you accomplish something that didn't seem feasible at the beginning? How can you affect people in such a way that they get up from their couches, send in music requests (at a fee), participate in sports events, and donate a lot of money to charity? One way is to do what the DJs from a Dutch radio station do every year at Christmas: lock themselves into a glass house (well, it's more of a container) without food and a minimum of sleep for six days, while collecting money for a good cause. For six days and nights, they can be heard live on the radio and seen on TV. Each time, their Serious Request event manages to select a worthy cause, that has great impact on the public and gets them to donate freely. No matter what kind of marketing expert you are, it's worth studying this case to see how an entire country gets caught up in the emotions this initiative triggers.

You see, they don't restrict themselves to playing music requests, they also organize auctions and get famous artists to perform in the container, for which the public pays generously. It's a true melting pot of modern media: radio is the main medium, supported by TV, the Internet, mobile apps, and print media. But Serious Request is much more. It's also a personal campaign by DJs who want to make a difference. Last year, one of the DJs staged a unique 'Circus Request' tour. He roamed the country and organized live performances in whatever theatre was available. Lots of artists donated their time, and once again, the public donated their money... One of the greatest things about this event is the radio station's boss announcing the revenues four hours before it ends. And then everyone feels compelled to break last year's record and puts in that extra bit of effort. As a result, more money is collected every year. Afterwards, the hungry DJs are freed from their glass prison and treated like heroes and the whole city celebrates.

It seems that nowadays, charities are better at campaigning than commercial organizations. Like Michael Porter, an American expert in the field of business strategy, summarized it: "Each strategy you deploy is about choosing to run a different race, with a clear goal ahead. That other race, which you had already decided to win in advance!"

Determining the goal is serious business, as the following example shows. On October 14, 2011 the new iPhone 4S was launched in the US. The goal was to sell four million in a single weekend. It was exactly one week after Steve Jobs' funeral and in the Apple stores they interpreted their mission with a smile: "Everyone who enters the store is asking for an iPhone 4S." And you say: "Of course I've got one for you," but in your head you can hear yourself think: "Hey, there goes another iPhone for Steve." The sales target was almost achieved: 3,999,999 phones were sold. Only 1 phone remained on the shelf. For Steve. The Apple myth lives on.

How do you create the attention curve for the goal you want to achieve? Don't regard it as something you can do on the side. Your energetic kick off and the soul you bring to it are the most important contributions you can make. Invest 90% in preparation and 10% in execution, don't leave anything to chance. The path to success still leads from the head to the heart and only then to the wallet ... Why don't you register as a volunteer with the Red Cross. Or are you going to contribute to one of the presidential campaigns in the US? Start learning, and above all start soaking up knowledge. Open your mind.

Pride, pleasure and preparation prevent a poor SM PERFORMANCE!

René C.W. Boender

Sports Heroes, Managers and the General Public Are All Addicted to SM...

Sportspeople can learn a lot from real top managers. And likewise, so-called managers can learn a lot from sports heroes and coaches. I have witnessed very funny presentations by both types of professionals: speed skater Johan Olav Koss, swimmer Pieter van den Hoogenband, and his greatest competitor, swimmer Ian Thorpe. One of these speeches was called *SM to the 4th power*, where the S stood for sports and the M for management. Meanwhile, SM is also used as an abbreviation of Social Media, and, granted, it can also refer to SadoMasochism. SM, SM & SM.

Being top of the bill in sports can hurt a lot, since working out and exercising often pushes sportspeople over the pain barrier. In that respect, it's a bit like SM. And that's just in training, because during the actual competition you don't feel any pain. Many top managers should try to engage in this kind of training a bit more and come up against the pain barrier once in a while. The fun should be injected back into your DNA, you need to become more aware of why you do things! For sportsmen, it's often that Olympic gold medal or becoming the champion of

the world. In the business world, the goal is no longer clear. Is it just about the profit? If that is so, then keep your fingers crossed and hope for a pleasant game, because the rest of the world will quickly get fed up with you, and that's the end of the game for you. Because "a business that makes nothing but money is a poor kind of business," as Henry Ford once said.

It's infinitely better to share your higher aspirations with everyone and state your goals, as a beacon on the horizon. Naturally, you need to have fun while working on it. Put yourself and your pride on the line in order to clarify your goals and prevent things from becoming unclear. On the other hand, pride is also your soul power, and you know this is invincible, even though you may get beaten once in a while. By acting like this you'll build up goodwill in your target group's collective memory. And the more goodwill the better. Preparing well in advance will prevent you from giving a bad performance. Because nowadays the bill is not only presented in TV interviews, sports programs or daily news shows. No, social media can make and break you too. That's when SM can really hurt you, more than you ever thought possible.

Make sure you know which letter (S or M) to bet on, before you feel the whip... Always respond to and engage with online messages, but teach yourself not to react to each and every comment. I've experienced these problems myself and I can tell you it's not easy to first count to 21 in such situations.

The 'BB' Spirit Is Gaining Ground, Everywhere, All the Time...

The present times, economically difficult as they are, have also led to a gigantic sense of reality, a new honesty is gaining ground all over the world and that's a good thing. It's called the 'BB' spirit, not as in 'BlackBerry' but as in 'Business Buddhism'. In *Great to Cool* we already predicted a shift from IQ to EQ, and subsequently to SQ, especially in business life. The Spiritual Q, the spiritual value of the things you're working on as a person or as a brand! Things that will make you a better person or brand, more committed and sincere, and true.

By reading Steve Jobs' biography in particular, the world has discovered how empowering it is to be well-balanced and above all to accept reality as it is. Such as death, even if it comes way too early. That's why we'll see a dramatic increase in the number of books about the power of doing business with SQ, and we can only applaud that. Because a bit more time for reflection and awareness won't do the business world any harm. Some entrepreneurs might open their eyes and realize that being in business starts with generosity and not business intentions! Isn't it strange that some companies are reporting high profit margins again, while the current economy is still stagnating? It seems as if we've already left the crisis far behind us, although everyone knows this can't be true. After all, we haven't changed our behavior. No way. We're exhibiting the same insane behavior that got us into trouble in

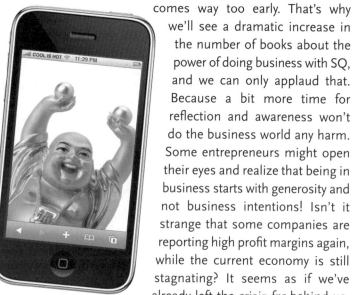

the first place. If we do not change fundamentally, it's just a matter of time before history repeats itself.

Buddhism teaches us how we can end the madness of our repetitive behavior of going around in circles ('samsara'): by doing away with ignorance. If we want to replace economically destructive behavior by economically sound and constructive behavior, we need to radically change things. This change of direction is necessary in order to feed the 9 billion people that will soon inhabit our planet. Even the Occupy Movement will need to change direction a bit and regain some trust in the goodness of people. That's why we're in need of a radical new view of the economy. We need 'Karmanomics', as Dutch trendwatcher and manager Kees Klomp calls it. Klomp links the Buddhist way of living to his worldly expertise as a former marketing and management advisor, as it were. He gives us very practical tips and tools for attaining personal, commercial and social well-being.

Now don't go thinking I've suddenly gone all vague and otherworldly! I'm not like that, my feet are always firmly planted on the ground. But by following the BB acceptance, I've started to look at things differently. You're probably thinking right now that you yourself are not vague either, but just think of Steve Jobs. He was a pretty cunning businessman but still adhered to a number of Buddhist principles. Sometimes, you just come across some principles that seem worthwhile to apply to your life. Just like you ignore other viewpoints, because they make you feel bad. The journey on the road to change has taken off because you've started seeing things differently, in a more balanced way. And wherever I present my views, I can feel that the SQ is gaining ground. That's what you want too, isn't it?

The road to business happiness is a rewarding journey.

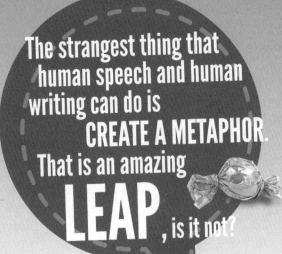

Keynote, X-mas or Kick-Off Speech: Endow It with Your Soul...

How can you lend wings to your kick-off speech? Do you manage to offer your audience the brain candies that go on to lead a life of their own? And who's going to write your speech? President Obama employs a top writer for the task, and the CEO of the Netherlands – our Queen – also employs people for this job.

But it's just as easy and much better to take some time and try to put something on paper yourself. Always reflect on what you want people to take away from the 3 minutes or so that you can claim their attention. Think of what you want them to be able to reproduce, after they've applauded you. Your fans won't really listen, because they're busy digesting the brain candies with their EQ. But meanwhile they might be tweeting precisely that one ambitious statement that matters. So always do a trial run and ask your audience what the net take away is. What's the net result, what do you remember?

The truth will come out anyway, once the press or the Twitter critics go public with their usually negative opinions. In less than 140 characters. This means the 3"12" rule is more applicable than ever. Don't be put off by the comments you may get, but use metaphors if possible. Believe me, John F. Kennedy's famous declaration "Ich bin ein Berliner" was no accident. Even if some linguists claim he mistakenly called himself a jelly doughnut. And what about "One small step for a man, one giant leap for mankind," uttered by the first man on the moon, or Obama's "Yes, we can!" None of these lines come out of thin air. Word wizards who are able to write great scripts have been working their butts off and have crunched their brains to come up with such slogans. "First dance, than think" does not apply to keynote talks, Christmas speeches, and kickoffs. "One more thing" was Steve Jobs' brilliant way of persuading his audience to keep listening.

The dumbest thing you can do in this respect, is grab an existing speech and edit it a bit, because you'll quickly be exposed as a fraud. But it's actually very smart to let yourself be inspired by the speeches of famous people like Barack Obama, Abraham Lincoln, Marie Curie, Mohandas Gandhi, Winston Churchill, Nelson Mandela, John F. Kennedy, Martin Luther King, Indira Gandhi, Mother Teresa, Václav Havel, and the Dutch Queen Beatrix. The Dutch monarch is getting more of a chance to speak her mind, and rightly so. In the old days, the court jester was a kind of spokesperson and critic of the king. The jesters have long since left the palace, but they have reappeared, on Twitter, and are apparently allowed to express all kinds of opinions.

Dare to touch on various topics in your speech, use the historic context and its influence on our history, and make sure you translate these things to future developments.

Since there are lessons to be learned from this, I've included some excerpts from Queen Beatrix's 2011 Christmas speech. It's straightforward and sincere, straight from the heart, and based on the principle that we should not only get, but above all give:

Many of us live in anxiety and insecurity about our existence. Unrest and concern for the future are predominant in Europe and in our country too. The worries are not only about individual prosperity, but also about our collective well-being and the way we are treating the Earth. Our precious planet is being treated carelessly, and what she gives us is unequally divided. Poverty and inequality are destroying the quality of life and are a threat to social solidarity. Selfishness and a craving for excessive wealth are blinding people to the harm that is inflicted upon our natural environment and undermining our civil consciousness. We have lost sight of the boundaries of what the Earth is able to provide, and of the sustainability of our society.

No country can prosper if its citizens are only concerned with their own gain. In assessing the value of all things, it is not only money that counts. Greed and self-enrichment are deforming the goal of the economy. We cannot ignore the needs of those who are not able to fend for themselves.

...

The numerous initiatives to practice all kinds of good intentions are encouraging.

...

Things that start out small have the ability to grow into a new culture of taking care of the future. Those who want to change the world, must start with themselves, evidently.

...

The challenge remains to do something yourself, together with others and with commitment to society. Everywhere, people are taking the initiative to live more conscientiously. This offers hope for a new perspective for the future. Especially young people encourage us to do so. With the strength of their convictions, courage, and self-confidence, they are seeking allies and inspiring their environment with a positive momentum.

Mahatma Gandhi once said: "Earth provides enough to satisfy every man's need, but not every man's greed." Since we are creatures that are endowed with reason and conscience, we can be expected to translate this principle into constant care for the Earth, and commitment to a just society.

Who could have written these beautiful words? The Queen herself? Actually, it doesn't really matter; you can sense this story has a soul, something personal. Twitter freaks will distil their own net take away from this, undoubtedly.

And that's what it's all about. How are you going to write your next kick-off speech and with who? Practice your speech, and remember: stay within 3 to 9 minutes, bearing in mind that the maximum length only applies to the really cool speakers! And don't forget to use the brain candy technique. By now, you've stored quite a few of these in your brain, I hope.

Hire Dream People and You Will Again Become a Business With a Story to Tell...

Don't let the bad times provoke you, this crisis will surely pass. At this very moment, opportunities are arising that can make you fly higher in the near future. Please don't let yourself be dragged down by negative views, don't let yourself be forced into believing other things than those that matter to you. Now is the time to hire precisely those people who still dare to dream: they are the best you can get. Remember, when all the other companies are letting people go, but you're hiring, you're actually successful.

On the whole, people who have a job are happier than people who are unemployed and who don't have enough to do to fill their days (or nights). Everybody has a right to work and you are in a position to create work. You might be thinking: "To tell you the truth, I don't need anyone at the moment." But let me tell you, you're wrong. You actually do need them. People with spunk, people who see things differently than your current staff. Employees who might want to open your car repair shop at 6.00 a.m. and start working right away. Or who are willing to do the necessary repairs at night, so the cabs and buses can start driving first thing in the morning without delay. In real life, a car dealer indeed started experimenting with night repairs and it became a big success. His turnover increased by 17%, and as a side effect, the number of cabs in the taxi cab business went up, which was also nice.

The great thing about hiring new people for a project or a limited period of time is that this doesn't necessarily have to cost you more in wages. A recent study in 25 Western countries showed that quite a large percentage of people (25%) prefer to have more leisure time. They would like to work one day or half a day less and are willing to give up about 10 to 20% of their wages in return. In the Netherlands, the progressive tax system ensures that your wages don't immediately decrease by the same percentage. Why don't you do the sums for your own crew. They will be much happier if they get what they want most: time off, even if it means sacrificing something and at the same time, giving others a chance.

For the company it means you can bring in fresh blood, new workers who want to go the extra mile, who are prepared to make an effort. This will enable you to advance your business case, while the rest are busy economizing. Everywhere you look, it's about slowing down. First it was slow food (a good idea). Next, it became slow living (not such a good idea), and finally people started to reject the concept of going to too much trouble and making an effort (even worse).

It looked like we had all the time in the world, but actually this was not true at all. So hurry if the following thought pops up in your brain: hey, this might be a good idea. Life's too short to mess about or spend time on irrelevant things. What would you write on your bucket list (10,000 things to do before you die)? What would you really love to do before you leave this Earth? Take a good look at information technologist Randy Pausch's final speech on YouTube. Here are some of his words.

What would you do if this was it? You have only one day to live. If today were your last day, you might tell someone you loved them. You might try to make amends with someone you had wronged. You might enjoy the time as much as possible. All of these things are good, but you can do them anytime. No need to wait for the warning of a last day that you'll never receive.

Most of us don't get the chance to know when our last day is, and even if we do, we're not usually in a position to make real changes.

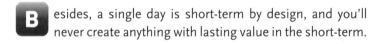esides, a single day is short-term by design, and you'll never create anything with lasting value in the short-term.

Sure, you can 'live in the present' – but if you want to build something beautiful, you'd better be thinking about the future as well. Instead of watching life as it passes you by, what if you actively worked on crafting a legacy composed of creative work that helps others?

What if there was a systematic method of 'legacy work' that allowed you to build this enduring record step-by-step? Yes, there might be plenty of time left. But what if there's not? There is an urgency to life, whether you want it or not. When you embrace the urgency instead of ignoring it, you can create something that changes the world. Oh, and you can do this in a fun way that makes the best use of your own talent and motivation.

In other words: don't sit in a corner and act like a sad little bird, but blow some air into your plans and make them fly. Before you know it, they will take flight and fly in the right direction...

May ICT Be with Us,
to Each of Us His Own PA...

For those who can still remember this: the Dutch coins (guilders) used to have the motto 'May God be with us' inscribed on their edge. The new euro had to do without this optimistic saying, and today we're feeling the consequences. In the present day it might be more appropriate to inscribe all the world's coins with the motto: 'May ICT be with us'. Because Information and Communication Technology makes life a whole lot easier. True, money has the same effect, but ICT has truly advanced matters dramatically. This enormous progress, often driven by the ICT-developing parts of the world, particularly India, China and Taiwan, will lead to an era in which computer systems, iPads, and even cell phones will become aware of their surroundings. Truly, your iPhone, BlackBerry, and Android phone will anticipate needs you weren't even aware of yet.

This latest trend will turn the information systems and service industry on its head for the next couple of years. The tide can no longer be turned, because the general public has embraced the smartphone and wants to make use of all the options and features of such a device. And if they don't carry their smartphones in their pocket, they have built-in communication technology in their new cars, such as the BMW with connected drive, but also in the TV sets you will soon be able to buy. For instance, the iPhone 4S is equipped with SIRI. This digital assistant is an indication of future developments, with a great amount of Steve's DNA in its genes. Ask SIRI a question and you'll get an answer. This will become a genuine sensation, especially when in the near future your Apple TV starts to respond to voice control, provided, of course, that it understands the language you speak. No need for remote controls any longer and you can watch exactly what you feel like watching...

Or imagine that your iPhone notices you have an appointment in New York at 7:15 p.m., but also sees that you're still somewhere in New Jersey. In that case, your iPhone can suggest postponing the meeting, all by itself, or remind you it's time to get into your car if you want to make the meeting. This technique even offers solutions for your personal safety, for instance if the roads have become slippery overnight and you simply have to catch your 7:15 flight. Your iPhone thinks your alarm is set a bit too late and decides to wake you up a bit earlier, so you'll have plenty of time to travel to the airport. Finally, everyone gets their own Personal Assistant, and one that goes a lot further than your regular PA. Although this new PA is discreet, it still looks over your shoulder and takes into account your private life, your wishes and the things your friends are interested in.

Apart from all this, your own PA will also become the filter that makes sure you don't waste your time watching nonsense. And it's about time, because at the moment more than 350 billion hours of digital video content can be found online. This staggering figure is expected to expand to 500 billion hours in 2015. It's impossible for any human being to digest that much information. No matter how much the world has changed, it's still impossible to cram more than 24 hours in a single day. Marketing expert Seth Godin nailed it perfectly in one of his vlogs: "As soon as you accept that just about everything in our created world is only a few generations old, it makes it a lot easier to deal with the fact that the assumptions we make about the future are generally wrong, and that the stress we have over change is completely wasted." And he's right: don't get stressed because everything changes so much and so quickly.

But you ought to get some serious stress if you've just realized that your company is not yet active in this field. Enjoy coming up with (ICT) solutions for people who would like to make their lives easier! Is that so difficult? Of course not. Smart and simple marketing starts with the apptitude that allows your own PA to organize your business and help you remember things that you otherwise might have forgotten.

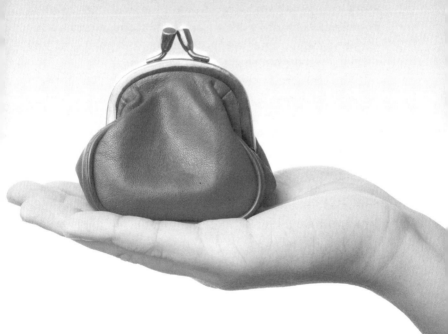

Apps Are 3" Door Openers.
So Start Making Life Easier...

Clearly, not taking part in the Appmania is an option, although if you choose this option, you risk not being found by your customers. Let's face it, 99.9% of all product searches start on the (mobile) Internet, and the quicker and easier people can find you, the better off you are. See it as a bicycle race. The first thing you do is explore the race track, right? And smart football players, or rather their coaches, always study their opponent's most predictable patterns, don't they? This truism has not been contradicted yet: he who is best prepared, wins the most! If you know the goalkeeper always dives to the right, you aim for the left-hand corner. It's a fact of life that the race is won by the person who crosses the finish line first, and you only score a touchdown if the ball ends up in the end zone.

Meanwhile, the newest apps go much further. Even if they're extremely commercial, they're still perceived as a kind of service by many users and their popularity is rapidly increasing, although you could say it's a way of Appvertising, actually. This is a very interesting market, especially for advertisers. The moment people actively start to look for a certain item and your brand or company pops up, even for a short while, you score points. Why? Because in that specific instant, you've made the consumer's life just that little bit easier. Let me illustrate this with the following example from the hotel industry.

Before you've even crossed the threshold, the hotelapp has already spotted you. Inside the hotel you won't find the receptionist, but a waiter who knows your favorite drink is an espresso, which he has already prepared for you. That's quite an entry, isn't it? The business of checking in has turned into the pleasure of having a quiet cup of coffee, so you feel immediately at home. If you might think "this is a bit over the top," try looking upon it as an act of ultimate customer pampering. It's close to getting intimate. And there are no hidden commercial motives; the cup of coffee is free of charge, because they appreciate the fact that you booked a room at their hotel again. In such a case you will experience this as an added bonus, and the hotel has created a repeat visit.

Incidentally, it's becoming quite crowded in app country. The genuine 'killer apps' were initially boosted by the traditional media who picked up on them and started to hype them, in the old-fashioned or the online newspapers. They fully exploited one of the indisputable truths about making contact: it's not about how far the medium can reach, it's always about reaching the people involved.

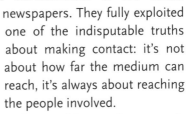

If something works out well, you need to maintain it, of course. An app needs to be innovated too, once in a while. You'll need to follow your app as if it were a regular ad, because an app has to be effective within 3", just like an ad. If you see that the public doesn't yet fully appreciate your app, then change course as soon as possible and don't wait until the race is over. Because afterwards, all you can do is evaluate what's gone wrong and wonder why your app ended up in the cemetery of deleted apps. Then, it will become extremely difficult to make your comeback with a new app.

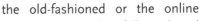y the way, you can justifiably compare an app to a regular product; if you keep optimizing your (on and offline) media exposure during the introduction phase of your product, you can achieve 12 to 18% more return, especially in the classic media mix, by continually adjusting the course. So, don't leave anything to chance, get to work right away. Even if you don't own a hotel, but a fashion boutique or an insurance company. Make life easier for your customers, since it's already difficult enough to simply survive...

Initiatives Deserve Commitment...

Somebody needs to make a start, but nobody is going to do it for you. Making plans is great fun, but remember, a plan is an inanimate object, it contains no energy; however, if you turn it into an initiative, it will gain momentum. It goes without saying that this initiative has to come from you. You need to pour your soul into it – make it personal, that is – if you genuinely want to reach out to the people involved. The truth of your words will come out in the behavior you exhibit, but first and foremost, in the tone you adopt. Today, being harsh is over, being real is hot. Men, in particular, will need to get used to the fact that we've entered the era of the sheconomy. This requires greater vulnerability and emotional involvement, and especially, being committed, with a clear goal to aim for. It certainly does not mean that you have to present yourself as a wuss, as women don't do this either. Although they use more skills than just the way they speak.

The power and influence of non-verbal communication will increase in the next few years. For example: how do you enter the conference room or hall? How do you shake hands with someone, provided this is allowed? Do you put on a friendly face, or do you frown in such a way that your audience can hear the thunder rumbling, without you having said a single word? You'll quickly discover that as soon as you change your attitude, your relations with others will also change. It is not necessarily to do with your appearance, although it helps if you look good. In the sheconomy it's not about the clothes you wear, or the way your hair is done. Beauty manifests itself in someone's non-verbal presence, and is especially reflected in their eyes. You see, eyes reflect what's really there, in someone's soul, and they are the door to someone's heart. The heart, as scientists have recently discovered, is the place where love resides. And when love comes into play, that's when commitment is at its greatest.

> Be naked, **OPEN YOUR SOUL** to someone! Let them into your spirit and share your **DREAMS**

Steve Jobs

What Do You Do Best?
Make Everything Magic ...

Some people have become so huge that it seems they have accomplished things that no human being can accomplish, and because of this they have become role models who inspire everyone's imagination. For example, Steve Jobs, who we all got to know a little bit better because of the wonderful books recently published and the videos circulating on YouTube. But do we actually, really know him? No, of course not.

Only when *The Truth About Steve* is published, on October 5, 2021, will we get to know Laurene Jobs' husband for real, from a first-hand account. Until then we'll have to make do with the different tales people tell about him, with the biography written by Walter Isaacson, former editor-in-chief of *Time Magazine*, at the absolute top of the charts.

In the near future we'll witness a large number of seminars on the subject of Jobs' way of doing business and on the key question: WWSD? Or, What Would Steve Do?

He was a true magician and it's a great pity that he can no longer take part in the revolution he brought about virtually on his own. He made sure that all kinds of products, in particular those manufactured by Apple, became more beautiful and user-friendly. He called it 'the Apple of his eye'. In spite of all the stories that are circulating, I know that he loved beginners' mistakes; you were allowed to make mistakes, provided you learned your lesson. As it happens, startups aren't yet burdened by being overcautious, by thinking 'I'd better not do this'! As writer and management expert Tom Peters put it so well: "If you're not prepared to be fired because of your belief in your current activities, you're working on the wrong project."

Jobs believed in his Apple, with heart and soul. Think big and act fast and make sure you're always a front-runner in this technological era: for Apple this is like performing at the highest level of professional sports. "Be the next big thing," and make sure the things you make get really big, too. While working on a project, you also need to dare to say 'no' to things that can distract you and throw you off the track to your higher goal. During *Time's Chicago Idea Week* conference, Bill Clinton told the audience that Jobs had said to him: "I don't think I have any weapons left, but I had a good time trying to beat it." He didn't believe he could fight his illness any longer, but he had enjoyed the fight. This is what he managed to write in preparation of a keynote speech that he sadly never got to present: "Beginners don't have baggage. You have nothing to lose. Don't live someone else's life. Think and Act Big. Be what's next. Put your heart and soul into it and have fun. Stay Hungry, Stay Foolish!"

Not a bad motto and good advice to apply to the things you're currently working on. Do you still have dreams? Or are you just defending your achievements and assets? Bring back the magic into your business, think of why you once decided to start your company and you'll see: Magic happens.

Finding Out Too Late...

One of the most common pitfalls in contemporary business life is looking back and enjoying your past achievements for too long. Of course, you're entitled to look back from time to time, to pat yourself on the back and enjoy the past. But don't linger too long, because the world keeps turning. On the other hand you could say we're not very good at celebrating success either, we don't pay enough attention to our achievements in business. Before you know it, you've made another mistake that keeps hounding you for years. We love to endlessly rehash stories about products, concepts and campaigns that failed (and about penalties missed in international soccer games, a sore spot in Dutch soccer history). Let's agree that it's a waste of energy to get stuck in these matters. You need to look forward instead and anticipate the necessary steps.

The worst frustration in modern day business life is undoubtedly the sense of discovering that it's too late once it's actually too late! Finding out that you've been on the wrong track for too long and you didn't have the sense to change. We often do this knowingly, and it will always remain a mystery why we do this. If you know it's going to hurt, it's better to endure a short, sharp pain than a prolonged, nagging pain. These times require clarity and honesty; they will build confidence and help you hold on to the trust your customers or organization put in you. It goes even further: vulnerability in leadership is as hot as can be. It's even perceived as cool when you admit to your

failures. Think of Bill Clinton's past 'adventures' and look at how popular he still is and has become once again. You're entitled to your mistakes, but don't make too many of them and please, never in front of the cameras. Making mistakes only demonstrates that you're strong enough to learn from your errors and you have a steep learning curve. Leaders who adopt this attitude better prepare themselves to enter the race for 'businessman of the year'.

Which project are you going to discard today? The project that will never succeed, as you know already? If you can't think of such a project you're a lucky devil. Does a project spring to mind? Then you know what to do. There are so many other things that need to be done...

Newspapers Become Cool Again...

How can you create the best possible platform for your product or service or for yourself? Without a platform your range is limited, it won't extend beyond your own scope. Although lots of people think that their job is done once they have made up a tweet and spread it among their followers, or created a website. Quite the opposite! You will need to prove that you are not talking nonsense, and you can be sure your audience will check this. We noticed this while we were researching Generation Z. We too were pleasantly surprised when we studied the reading behavior of Generation Z kids and found out where they do their fact-checking.

It's a mistake to think that the golden oldies don't matter anymore in the current day and age. Especially those newspapers that have been known for years for their independent viewpoints are still regarded as authorities. Because they still take the time to check whether a news item is true or not. The Z youngsters are very good at finding enormous amounts of sources for all kinds of gossip and trivia, but news has to be based on facts, and has to be accompanied by opinions, if desired. Fact and fiction can't be mixed up and to prevent this you need some kind of filter. Now we all know that *The New York Post* often finds it difficult not to go for the sensationalist headlines, but newspapers such as *The New York Times* and the *Washington Post*, and *Time Magazine* too, usually manage to distinguish fact from fiction.

Evidently, we must never allow Thomas Jefferson's prediction to come true: "The advertisement is the most truthful part of a newspaper." Although the advertisements tend to add a certain flavor to the paper, making it more lively and attractive. The news and the traditional newspaper (or their 24/7 website) prove to be the best medium to inspire and activate people. It's the ideal platform to get as close as possible to the consumer's purchasing moment, all the more so if you combine your actions with appvertising. That is to say: try to be present at the exact spot where things are starting to happen. The starting point always has to be 'making contact', preferably in mere seconds. Such a starting point is crying out for creativity and that's exactly where you can excel. The more creative you are, the better.

It will probably cost you, but it will benefit you even more, especially if you manage to grab the public's attention with so-called topical ads that highlight a certain content or event. On the Internet you can find all sorts of calendars with various events that are suited to this kind of advertising. For instance, the Super Bowl, the NBA Championship, Lollapalooza music festival and the Olympic Games. These events have already proven their added value in the past and are securely stored in our collective memory. It seems that these developments are once again directing attention to the newspapers and news networks that employ independent editors, making them the focal point of independent news provision. TV shows often come by their news items by reading the papers, or trawling YouTube, since these are the media where the newsworthy discussions take place, where the people of interest are discussed. After their appearance on TV, they really start to become famous and cool.

It's a game, but one in which you can't afford to be sloppy. You must be very accurate. Anyhow, you can rely on certain newspapers to provide truthful information. So don't let other types of media make you crazy. Take a good look at your own media mix. How is it put together? Why don't you put it back into the mixer again and try to plan things by following your intuition, the old-fashioned way...

> Our goals can only be reached through a vehicle of a plan, in which **WE MUST FERVENTLY BELIEVE,** and upon which we must vigorously act. There is no other route to **SUCCESS**

Pablo Picasso

Chart a Clear Course!

A name indicates what we seek. An address indicates where it is. A route indicates how we get there. That's all there's to it. You waste the most time by engaging in endless and useless discussions, and above all, by continuing to doubt the chosen path to success. Remember that you can't possibly manage something if you aren't able to give a clear description of it. Choosing your destination, the place where you want to arrive, is the most important decision in the process of getting from A to B. And of course, you're going through all this trouble to be able to successfully cope with the world again, full of energy.

Clear signposting – statements explaining how you think you'll get there – is essential. Just like the road signs or the traffic signs at the airport. Ambiguous or indistinct signs on the way to the airport will result in chaos and will lead to a lower score on the Customer Satisfaction Index of this particular airport route. A clear path will also clear your head and people will be prepared to follow the path, knowing that it is the quickest way to their destination. But they'll definitely want to know why this is the right way, especially the women within your organization. Well, naturally, the new type of man, driven by his EQ, will be curious about that too.

In fact, anyone has a right to a distinct path, in business life as in politics. That is why a strategy always needs to be clear; after all, it is the starting point for all ideas, and people like to contribute. We think in order to act, but we definitely act in order to think, that's a given truth. So cut the crap and start making some sense! And absolutely put an end to developments that are no longer of value to you and which are headed towards certain disaster. Above all, accept 100% responsibility for your own proven added value. Dare to make a stand in this process and act as a surefooted GPS on the road to the future. Don't forget that every organization only starts to make money at the end of the chain. This means you always have to arrive at your destination if you want to cash in. So make sure everyone in your organization realizes this, support the weakest link in your organization during this process or replace this link if need be.

Make use of your talents, leave your comfort zone far behind and rediscover the opportunities that present themselves in this specific era. Do it right away, because these days, opportunities don't abound. What do you intend to do to signpost the right path even clearer to your employees? Oh yes, and don't forget to record your story with your mini FLIP camera as you go along, so you can show it to your online customers right away.

The clearer the path, the more customers will find you. And the more they find you, the more successful you will become...

The New Freedom: Organize More DIY…

It's hard to imagine, but some of us are happy with things the way they are, with the status quo. Others prefer to keep discovering new and different ways of doing things. Personally, I think the latter is the wiser option. Because of the way the stock market reacts, and the so-called crisis we're in at the moment, the following is a truism: "Now you own it, now you don't!"

The new reality is defined by the situation as it is now, not as it used to be. "Until politicians actually do something about the world economy, be afraid!" Still, fear has never been a good counselor and you can't expect the politicians to solve everything. Let's not forget that we are the ones who elect our governors and senators. In my opinion the starting point is to realize that things can't go on like this any longer. Not only on a global scale, but also in our own environment and in our own company, because there too, we'll need to embrace the big change.

As I said before, five years ago it wasn't such a bad time at all, and it's absolutely not true that our situation has improved dramatically year by year. Of course, it's not exactly thrilling to notice your spending power is slowly deteriorating, but there are more important things in life. Partly, this mindset is something you're talking yourself into: once everybody starts investing more energy in building a new reality, everyone will start to feel a lot better too. Freedom is crucial in that respect. As I mentioned before, lots of people are prepared to sacrifice 20% of their work time and work fewer hours in order to give others a chance on the job market, even if some decision-makers would have us believe otherwise.

That's because work makes people happy and gives their lives a sense of purpose, especially since the new way of working is gaining ground (and this time, it's not just words, as it was when insurance companies used to pay lip service to it). No, it's really going to happen this time: the big revolution is imminent now that labor and money are going to be divided more equally among the population. The 21st century demands that we change our 20th century organizational structures right now, not to mention our leadership styles that often date back to the 19th century. New leaders give their people freedom and trust. The people of today and tomorrow, Generation Z, are much more competent and able to organize their lives and also their work. Home and work increasingly blend and today's workers are capable of managing this excellently. They no longer have any need for the old organizational structures or some kind of feudal manager. In fact, they won't even work for such companies! You know, those companies that don't understand that people who work at home are often more productive than those who hang out at the office all day long, even though you can't 'manage' such home workers every minute of the day.

Given the labor shortage we'll be facing in the near future, it might be a good idea to make haste with redesigning your organization; make it a matter of life and death! Hurry now you've still got time, because it'll give you some spare time (and a head start) while the others are still scrambling to adjust to the new rules of the game. Above all, give your people lots of responsibility and you'll see that they will take their task seriously. They will go the extra mile and inspire others to do that too. It's the standards that determine whether the goal is achieved, not the so-called rules. The rules merely exist to be broken. So you will also need to break off all sorts of linear processes, and instead give free reign to freedom, a lack of hierarchy, and complexity! And you will have to start changing course towards more freedom in effectiveness and innovation (Do It Yourself), in order to become better and better by using great ideas. That will certainly give you an energy boost...

> A good ad which is not run never produces sales, **NO SOCIAL MEDIA** means missing all **CONTACTS**
>
> Imelda van der Helm

Beware of the Social Media Blooper...

The late baby boomers are the fastest growing group, if you look at the people who have recently started using social networks. In particular, the rapid growth of tablet computers has got this group using social media in massive numbers, and they're loving it. They're discovering the medium that comes naturally to the Generation Z kids, and the same goes for Generations X and Y: the NOWCONOMY is here. Although NOW is in fact a SHEconomy, as I said earlier. Everyone wants everything and right at this moment! Add the Appmania to this mix: install and run the software and the party can get started. Don't worry, it's not as complicated as you think, you just need to find out how it works. A straightforward workshop can enlighten those who still are a bit afraid of SM, and help them on their way. But let it be clear that you have to start using SM, before you really start hurting.

As of now, nobody is exempt and everybody is present on the web. Without exaggerating we can presume that it has become a vital necessity of life. Young, old, male or female, no matter what their social status or wealth, they all use social media. Nevertheless, somewhere in the distance we can still catch a glimpse of a large group of people for who Social Media is still an unknown concept. Strange but true, it's the CEOs of various companies we're referring to! Even now, some of them are afraid to get their feet wet in this unique medium. Although business leaders are increasingly making use of platforms such as Facebook, LinkedIn and Twitter, they aren't doing so because it's cool but only because they can't afford not to. They still aren't aware of the advantages of these new means of communication. We're really talking about a missed opportunity here and it's high time for a wake-up call.

You see, social networks are a very powerful tool in influencing, expanding and tightening the bonds with all sorts of people. Using social media might even be the last straw in terms of sales figures. This is the deal: social media not only influence the way in which we communicate, they also give the 3"12" boost. So don't look upon this type of communication as the marketing department's latest trendy toy, because using this medium will have an impact on all sectors of the company. Almost every department, from human resources to product development, can profit from the benefits that social media have to offer. This also goes for CEOs and board members. Using social media can offer them enormous advantages, although there are some negative aspects too.

However, social media's bright side more than outweighs their dark side and ignoring this communication channel is no longer an option. Social media can close the gap between the board of directors and the workplace, they can keep you, as a CEO, informed of what the online community is saying about your company and your products, and they can give you useful tips on how to influence public opinion or how to put your brand or your personality to good use for your company.

After all, you make the difference, especially if you decide to take action. If you don't feel safe yet using SM, let the experts teach you how to do it. They aren't difficult to find. If you use the social media, that is. Just ask the crowd in the cloud. And otherwise you can always send me an e-mail, I'll be happy to tell you where you can find the best courses and training, which will open a whole new world to you.

Open the New EQ Perspective and Focus on Change...

The new way of working will cause everything to change, in particular staying on at work after you've retired. By now, most people have realized they'll have to keep on working after they've reached the age of 67 – or even 70 – but nevertheless it's still a nightmare to them. Doing the same thing each and every day just doesn't feel right, unless you're an artist or a comedian. Although they will also need to open their minds to the 3,1,1 idea!

In future, holding more than one job, with the different social environments that go with these jobs, will become a status symbol. This is a fact of life for Generation Z, but let's be honest: wouldn't you rather work your regular job for three days, spend one day doing something you've always dreamed of, and use the last day to engage in useful social activities with your best friends, because the tedious chores need to be done too, after all.

3,1,1 is going to be the new working style, intended to break through the routine, and above all, to hang on to the labor force necessary to keep our country going. Nobody can escape this new world, since everyone has become some kind of Big Brother and everything is visible to everyone else nowadays. While Berlusconi was only slaughtered in the traditional media, we might find ourselves being destroyed in the social media as well. You can clearly sense the hardening of the debate in these media, as demonstrated by *The Economist*'s headlines regarding Berlusconi: "The man who screwed an entire country!" This continued to be a subject of intense debate on the social media forums for a long time.

Currently, for *Time Magazine,* the person of the year is the protester; actually, that's all of us. So it's best to focus on a single thing: yourself. Make sure that you are in tune with yourself and do the things you've always dreamed of doing, at least for one day a week. From now on, the basic rule is: get back to the good old times of courtesy to stay ahead! Simply be yourself and be open and approachable. Focus on the 3,1,1 future for your extended working life up to the age of 70, and on vulnerability in leadership. Try to understand more, but not everything; as you'll never understand why a woman needs to have eleven handbags or 80 pairs of shoes. Unless you've understood the ultimate truth about women: a bag is the only accessory any woman can wear, no matter what size she wears. You see, handbags don't need to follow a diet!

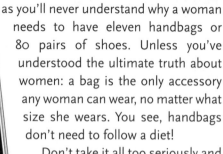

Don't take it all too seriously and play along. Cool fashion is not just about buying stuff: it's part of the job of being a (wo)man, that's what they say in fashion circles. By the way, skin care products for men are the fastest growing category in personal care these days. And we also own more pairs of shoes than ever before. Get used to these changes as quick as you can, and then everything will start getting better. You'll see!

The Pop-Up Store Presents Opportunities for Innovation…

Are we still able to think small? Do we still know what it feels like to crank up the engine ourselves? And do we still feel like doing it? If you're wealthy enough to be able to afford doing nothing, then please read on, because we really need your money to keep our businesses going. If you're less well-off, tear out this page and find out what you can do to play your own economic games and create your own mini-economy. Yes indeed, there are all sorts of opportunities to start a business, but you'll have to do it yourself. In the end, that's why the Chinese are so powerful; they don't sit around waiting for government support, since there is no such thing in China. Instead, they are encouraged to do the things they would like to do.

In the Western world, we've been dependent on government support for too long, even in starting up our companies. It was great for those who could benefit from it at the time, but it won't help you at present. Subsidizing the economy can wear out a company, and a company that is worn out will be less energetic. So never again ask for grants, but ask for a loan if necessary to do what is essential: start up.

The world around us is changing rapidly. There are more empty retail premises than ever, which does not look good in a shopping mall and reflects badly on the atmosphere and the turnover of the surrounding shops. A solution was offered by a company that came up with a great idea to remedy these vacancies: they pasted various stickers on the empty shop windows, just to let the public know that something was actually going on there. All at once, the street looked a lot better, and the shop looked taken care of. Believe it or not, prior to the sticker action, the building had been unoccupied for 13 months, but two months later, the premises were rented out again. Coincidence?

Here's another example. Since business was a bit slow for a catering company, the owner thought: why not call the owner of that empty store in my street and ask him if I can use his shop for four days to open a Valentine's Day Pop-Up restaurant. They made a deal to link the rent to the turnover and bingo!, another hit was born. For four days, the 'love restaurant' was completely sold out. The turnover was quite good too, and the street had been revitalized. The town council even wants to grant a catering license to that premise! Coincidence? No, because this event was the centre of attention in Twitterland for a while and having dinner there became a real hype.

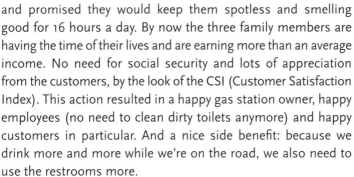

In short, there are loads of opportunities for making a profit, as long as your idea has added value. How about this: a gas station along the highway always had smelly, dirty restrooms. A family of who several members were unemployed asked the gas station owner if they could exploit the toilets and promised they would keep them spotless and smelling good for 16 hours a day. By now the three family members are having the time of their lives and are earning more than an average income. No need for social security and lots of appreciation from the customers, by the look of the CSI (Customer Satisfaction Index). This action resulted in a happy gas station owner, happy employees (no need to clean dirty toilets anymore) and happy customers in particular. And a nice side benefit: because we drink more and more while we're on the road, we also need to use the restrooms more.

Here's another example of a mini-economy in the shape of a Pop-Up activity. A hotel somewhere in the south was visited by an unemployed, highly educated young man who asked if he could wash the guests' cars at night. By hand, with a neat display card on the hotel's reception desk: "Get your car washed while you sleep, just $ 9.95. Cleaning of interior for an additional $ 5.00". He started work at 10:30 p.m., and on the first night he washed three guests' cars and the staff's cars. After a week, his business had grown and he had to wash 15 cars a day/night, and if this keeps up he will have as many as 25 to 39 cars daily. Wow, what a great Pop-Up turnover, created all by himself! Payment was simply combined with the hotel bill, and the customers were glad they could use this extra service. You could tell by the numerous positive tweets and the higher CSI rating by the hotel customers.

The emergence and development of new, interactive means of communication will lead to changes in consumer demands. It puts certain items on the agenda: agenda-setting, as it is called in the marketing business. Carrying out Pop-Up ideas and using social media to market them is a great challenge, but also creates great opportunities for the business world. In particular, opportunities to revitalize existing business processes and make them more efficient, more effective, and more profitable. Because social media don't just influence the way in which individuals communicate with each other, they influence all layers of society. Everybody is affected by this new means of communication on a daily basis. Consumers, employees, and most certainly customers, will not only become more empowered, but will also make different demands of companies, brands, products, methods of communication, distribution and sales. And in any area where the Pop-Up concept can save people some time, you'll be rewarded with a growing turnover. How are you going to use the Pop-Up?

Just Do It in 24 Hours...

The usual daily routine is becoming a bit old-fashioned in this era of flexible working hours. If you prefer to start work at 5:30 a.m. to avoid traffic, by all means, do so; if you prefer to start a bit later and work late, after office hours, please do. But don't forget to set a limit to your working hours. Before you know it, you won't be getting enough sleep and you'll keep grinding on. Just one more e-mail to send, one last document to check, oh, don't worry, i'll take care of this tonight... Sound familiar?

Don't forget that your iPad, iPhone or notebook comes with an on/off button and you're the one who decides whether the device is switched on or off. Nobody is indispensable 24 hours a day. It still hasn't been proven that you can cram more than 24 hours in a single day, and faster than the speed of light is still not possible. Until conclusive evidence has been found to the contrary, Einstein is still right. Even if neutrinos are about 60 nanoseconds faster than the speed of light while traveling a distance of 453.6 miles, this doesn't amount to a lot of time saved, at least not to us humans. So try to find the balance in your life, because these days, 'work hard, play hard' emphatically requires 'rest hard' too!

It's a knack, and a new way of living, to do this in a way that lets you enjoy life fully while also using your talents to your potential. Do you want to spend time with your kids, from 3:30 p.m. until they go to bed? Then do so, and switch the TV off for a change. Would you like to work out in the afternoon and feel refreshed in the evening? Do it, and leave your cell phone in the gym locker! But mainly, don't do everything half-hearted, put your heart in it and commit yourself 100%. This also goes for when you rest, since getting some rest is often forgotten. Why don't you practice yoga for half an hour, listen to your favorite music or go for a walk. At any rate, distance yourself a little from the 24-hour race you're competing in all the time. Generation Z uses the word 'chill' for this phenomenon. The older generation might take this for hanging around without being of much use to anybody, but it's better to regard this as a way of recharging your batteries. These kids are looking for a balance in their lives in order to perform better.

Is that what you do too? Work is just a game, the rest, i.e. life, is serious. A healthy mind in a healthy body will achieve more than a tired, burned out and exhausted worker, who is much too hard on himself. What are you going to do now? Put this book aside and go for a walk? Or are you so excited that you want to go on reading now? Both are excellent choices, as long as you have consciously and deliberately made a decision to do whatever you're going to do...

We're Consciously Moving from Eating Less to Eating More Often, but Tastier...

If there is one sector in which life never stops, it's the food business. Still, that's where the biggest change of all times is imminent, a switch that we'll discuss later on. It's a truism: no matter what, you'll always need food and drink, otherwise you can't survive. You might be shocked at how much you eat and drink during the day; in the Western world, the average person consumes about 3.5 lbs of food and drink a day. The following morning, you say goodbye to some seven ounces when you visit the toilet. Shit! Is that all? Yes, that's all you lose after consuming three and a half pounds of food and drink.

Hopefully you burn off the rest by doing the things you love, such as working, exercising, playing sports and living life to the fullest. In the past few years, the three fixed meals a day have been replaced by about seven dinner/lunch moments. We're starting to resemble the Asians more and more. They eat far more often, although they don't eat bread but always a hot snack. Even in the morning. We've started drinking our breakfast much earlier, because we need to catch a train or we want to avoid traffic jams, and around 10 a.m. it's time for a nice cup of coffee with a bite of something. The only moment that still seems to be fixed, all over the world, is our midday lunch. Nearly everyone stops for lunch at noon, but afterwards we all differ in when we stop for our next bite. At 4 p.m. it's time for the famous cup-a-soup moment, although we've cut down on the salt and we don't throw a fit like in the hysterical Dutch TV commercial. Later on, we have dinner, and then at around 8 p.m. we drink coffee and especially tea. At 10 p.m. our stomachs beg us for the familiar late-night snack!

Because of this high frequency, the meals we eat have all become smaller and around 1.4 ounces lighter, which leads the experts to believe that by the year 2015 we'll have cut down on our meals substantially. In the US, it's hot now to have lunch-sized meals at dinner time, and two instead of three courses. Strangely enough, the current generation (Z) is the healthiest ever, but at the same time they're also the fattest. I think the problem is breakfast; if we'd just go back to eating one or two slices of bread instead of only drinking a glass of juice, we wouldn't go out the door on an empty stomach. We'd start our day in a healthier way; even better, you'd usually eat six times a day instead of seven. By the way, some dentists don't approve of eating meals so often, because the food attacks your teeth six times a day instead of three; but that's why they invented the toothbrush, right?

Where am I going with this story? Well, these new eating habits offer employers and caterers a great opportunity to introduce 'early morning breakfast' at work. A nice, early, healthy start of the day, no traffic jams in sight. Instead of eating cookies during the meeting you could bring fruit snacks and put those out at the reception desk too, where visitors will see them right away. Not only is it much healthier, it looks a lot fresher.

What are your own eating habits? Which course could you skip and feel a lot better? It may seem like a drop in the ocean, but you'll notice that everybody feels more refreshed. Why don't you change to six healthy meals a day, and implement that change at your company and at home as well. After all, food always tastes best at home...

We TRAVEL,
some of us forever, to seek other states, other lives, other souls...

Anais Nin

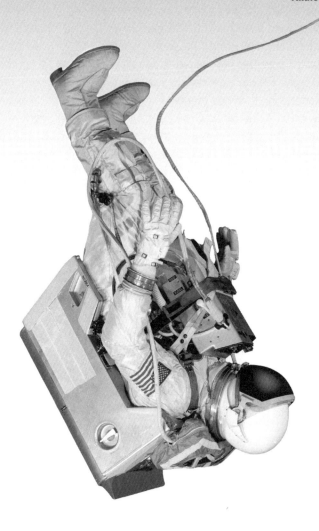

The New Travel Season Has Begun...

Richard Branson's Virgin will fly us into space and soon to Australia, within 3.5 hours. Or will Dutch KLM win this competition? My chauvinistic heart might think it's going to be KLM, but deep down I sense the winner will be Sir Richard. If you had to name an industry that has been at the forefront of finding new uses for ICT, then it would be the aviation and travel business. They helped make our world smaller and smaller and we don't even need paper tickets any longer. Do you still recall the first time you took off for the airport without clutching an actual airplane ticket and how nervous you were about it? All you had to do was say your name and you were amazed that everything worked out fine! Which meant that you were allowed on board, no problem. This has become commonplace nowadays.

But this very same head start seems to be vanishing quickly, now that certain ICT systems appear to be built to annoy us customers. Have you ever had to pay $ 80 in transfer costs because your first initial on the ticket was incorrect? Entering the data again takes less than a minute and (over)charging your passengers for this service frustrates them tremendously. The airlines that still have such a policy really need to lower this fine to about $ 7.50, which is a realistic price for the service. They should bear in mind that it doesn't take an angry customer long to mention their name on Twitter, and that will cost them a lot more...

Social media have lent wings to the travel business and made it more transparent. You can quickly find out all sorts of things about any destination, any hotel and even any restaurant you like. This means your image is actually your Internet amigo. The friendlier you are, the better you'll do. You know, this new revolution is also the greenest one imaginable. We're saying goodbye to stacks of paper travel guides once and for all and display an animated guide on our iPad or iPhone instead. We no longer need to cut down trees and we can watch lifelike images of our destination. All you need to do is make sure your guide and your pictures on the Internet are up to date. And don't you try to hype such a guide through a viral, as was the fashion for a while. Of course, a viral is always an option, but often unnecessary. If the product is authentic, it will automatically find its way to the brain position.

G enuine content will always be noticed and travels by itself. The crap, which is there as well, will end up buried in the Internet cemetery, in ruins. Take a look at IKEA, with their catalogues. Although the paper catalogue has become a collector's item, you can view many more products online. In the meantime, other large mail order companies, such as Sears and Conrad Electronic, have published their catalogues online or will let you download their entire catalogue as a PDF file.

Of course you can pull this off too, whether you're active in the food industry or in some other business. Why don't you collect every possible picture of the products you sell that your suppliers can provide. Publish them in an e-magazine and the content will travel straight to the brain. Because nowadays, traveling is more than just being on the move. Which destination are you going to choose?

You Seduce People Because of Who You Are...

It's always important to radiate personality, to be someone. You are either something or you are nothing; you're pleasant, or fast, or even better, you're both. The more positive the first 3" of personality recognition the better. People prefer to work with positive people rather than with a sourpuss who thinks everything is way too much trouble. It's exactly the same with a brand. And now we're talking brand personality. If you have it, cool. If you don't, then start working on it.

Before you have uttered a single word, your public should already have an image in mind that's relevant to your product, that charges your product. The giant Disney cartoon company has accomplished this with the words Magic and Kingdom. Can you think of a similar example for your own company? Think this over and try to develop your own vocabulary. By using the right language you can create desire and seduce the customer into making a choice, because you see, everyone loves to have a choice. A choice of one is no choice at all and will be seen as something negative in the long run. That's why you should always be glad to have some competition. It will keep you on your toes and present the customer with a wider choice and an opportunity to choose one over the other. A long time ago, you were a fan of the Rolling Stones, while your brother preferred the Beatles; some people love Coca Cola, while others prefer 'a new generation'. Pepsi, that is.

You need to have the courage to surprise and change in order to keep conquering. This battle for the consumer's favor is good for anybody's personal growth and leads to innovation. This is clearly demonstrated by the recent fights between Apple and Google, now they have become outright competitors of the Android system. Or would Samsung or LG emerge as the winner? Unless Microsoft and Nokia have managed to find the reset button.

There are many paths you can take if you want to seduce the customer and charge your brand personality. Like Microsoft, for example, they tried to dominate the markets for a long time, but now they've changed tack and are trying to operate in a different manner. Google and Apple use the strength of their product a lot more, and while Google parades its openness, Apple is much more reserved (which many people find appealing) but flaunts its product design. Actually, Apple sells 'a way of life and a way of being'. One is sexy, while the other tends to be a bit geeky. By following both brands for a while you can learn a lot that you can then apply to your own situation. Let's call it Appleism versus Googleism, for some people they are true religions. This street university education enables you to learn from the best marketing experts, who you can follow without paying a dime.

And the ultimate highlight is the Consumer Electronics Show in Las Vegas. This gigantic international electronics fair is where the latest gadgets and innovations are presented. If you have the opportunity, you should surely visit this fair and soak up the atmosphere, let yourself be inspired. Who would you like to be, which brand or company would you like to own? Take a good look at their business case and their marketing style. If you make a choice, others will automatically choose you, and this way you will also charge your own brand! It comes down to this: who are you, or who do you want to become? It will never change: there are those who need to sell, and others who are bought. That's why I prefer to be the other.

Anyone who thinks that they are **TOO SMALL TO MAKE A DIFFERENCE** has never tried to fall asleep with a **MOSQUITO** in the room.

Christie Todd Whitman

Hurry, Make the Big Decision!

Lots of people efface themselves and think they're too small to take big steps. Rubbish, bull. After all, small is the next big thing. Little Randy Newman became a great musician, didn't he? Stop underestimating yourself or the company you work for. Whatever you do, think back to the mosquito in the brain candy on the previous page. Read it once more, aloud, so loud that your wife, husband, kid and even your dog wonder what the ..bleep.. you're doing, to which you reply: "I'm reading a brain candy." Okay, now just assume that with all the new technologies and possibilities, the whole world has become your working area. Whether you're heading in a certain direction just this once or have fundamentally changed your course, at least let everybody know. You need to take matters into your own hands and make sure that the world focuses on you and can actually find you.

Everybody needs to learn to walk before they can run. In other words: we all started out small and learned our skills along the way. Although after a while you need to be ready to take big steps; if you have a truly great idea, don't take it to market in a small way. Understand that your time is limited and that you need to be just in time. Neither too late, because then you'll come off second-best, nor too early, because you will be too far ahead of your time. The moment your SQ tells you you've really got something here is the exact moment you should spring into action. This goes for politicians too. Let's be honest, it's nonsense to wait until 2020 to raise the retirement age. It's better to do this as soon as possible. That will provide clarity and everybody will know where they stand. It goes without saying that this active attitude is also badly needed in business life. Be distinct and explain which path you're following, chase away the fog that surrounds your ideas and clearly state your opinions.

For instance, if you own a successful business and you're

asked time and time again to turn it into a franchise, which you absolutely loathe, then make this clear on your website. This will prevent others from wasting time and energy in trying to persuade you and it will also save you a lot of time. The British *Pret a Manger* sandwich shops are a good example of this method. Their website states it very clearly, you can't miss it: "Franchising, sorry we don't. Please don't call us and ask for a franchise because we don't. We really don't! The fact is, we don't like to franchise, so we won't." This demonstrates how honest, clear communication can work, or rather, how it should work!

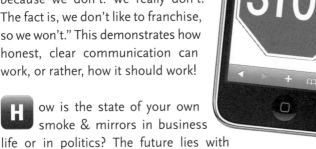

How is the state of your own smoke & mirrors in business life or in politics? The future lies with honesty, and it really doesn't matter if you're a big fish or small fry. As long as you make clear decisions.

Evolution
is not a force but a process.
Not a cause BUT A LAW

John Morley

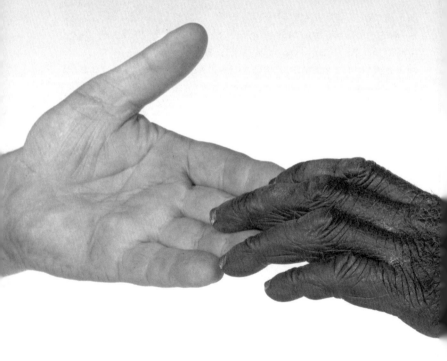

Make the Switch

Some trends are just unstoppable and while you may oppose them you already know it's just putting off the inevitable. This is quite understandable and logical, since it's so convenient to keep doing what you've always done. But when there is no further growth and you even expect things to get worse, you'll actually have to change course! If you are competing in such a race, against your better judgment, and have stopped growing, you may be able to hold out for a while longer; but by today's standards you're already on the way out. In that case, you could try to follow the advice below.

Go on an 'idea-safari' to learn from experiences in other lines of business, and then try to apply this knowledge to your own field. Think about the revolution in the supermarket sector, where first the shopping basket and then the shopping cart started a real revolution when they were introduced 35 years ago. Nowadays, you can stick your iPad on your cart, so it can suggest which groceries to buy while you're racing through the aisles. Because we'll spend less and less time shopping for groceries and the food buying process will become faster and faster. Although some smart supermarkets have started to cook fresh meals inside the stores. This makes the store smell great and attracts more customers, who go in just for fun. People walk in and smell delicious wok meals; even Walmart and Kroger have started to pay attention to fresh foods and supply recipes and healthy food tips. McDonald's, too, wants a slice of this kind of business to get the chardonnay girls to come inside.

If you think about it, it's weird that the restaurants in this world see all this happen, but don't do a thing to lure people back into their inns and taverns. Isn't this a chance to make a new start? Or will it be up to the caterers to bend the foodservice industry around towards a form of 'coordinated catering'? It might even be the foodservice industry itself that starts developing concepts for their own food sales and shortens the food chain by removing the restaurant link. And some sort of fusion may spring up between caterers and foodservice suppliers, which will introduce a type of fusion sales, akin to fusion cooking. Anyhow, something's got to give, since the number of businesses is rapidly decreasing and the number of self-employed people is growing explosively.

What will smart caterers do with these developments? Well, they will step outside, even beyond their comfort zone! They're well aware that the food business has become a very crowded marketplace where prices are permanently under pressure. The 'grazing consumer' is increasingly on the move and therefore out of the house; even if they have an excellent corporate cafeteria, they still seem to think that food eaten outdoors always tastes a little bit better. The seven snack-size meals a day (or maybe six, if it's up to you) will increasingly be eaten outdoors. In the US there are some traveling chefs who prepare and sell great gastronomic dinners from their vans. The new food culture will surely bring about a switch in the food chain, particularly for young Generation Z workers who will soon start claiming jobs. But the older generation too, those who continue working when they've reached retirement age, will discover how easy it is to eat healthy meals outside the home, and they will easily make the switch!

In what way can you take advantage of this situation? Because one thing is for certain: we are all human, so we must eat in order to survive...

Be Brief, Make It Simple

Of course, not in personal or telephone conversations or encounters. There you need to take your time to really make contact. But since almost anything on the Internet starts with a smartphone, we'll see new rules emerging as to how you spell and enter your name. Everything starts with an impulse, an idea; even if nobody can remember what the initials originally stood for, everybody recognizes them subconsciously.

IBM, IKEA, H&M, BMW... everybody knows them. Most of the successful brand names are abbreviations, or they consist of just one or two syllables: Shell, Esso, Apple, Senz, Jumbo, ZARA, Starbucks. This way, even virtually unpronounceable names are easier to remember. Actually, this is a gift of our desire for speed, initiated by Twitter users, who want to use as few characters as possible to convey what and who they are talking about.

The language will change drastically too: best regards has now become BR. Let's take the rest of this sms/Twitter/turbo language for granted, even if linguists aren't very happy with it. Nowadays it's also hot again to include digits in your name, or add them to a name to indicate a new type or model, as was the fashion in the late 1980s and the early 1990s. Back then it was internet provider XS4all, for instance. Now it's all about the iPad3, the IPhone 4S, and the BMW 3, which will probably prompt BMW to call its convertible the BMW 4 when it's launched. That's because people are looking for something solid, and they like to know what they're going to buy, or have just bought. Some brands need to make a big effort to sell, while others are simply bought. Just look at how Coca Cola, by now called Coke almost everywhere, has attached a whole new meaning to the word 'zero'.

That's the way it is; people love some kind of peg by which they can easily remember you, be it a well-known color code or a pay-off line. A pay-off line is a slogan that communicates what the brand stands for, briefly and to the point. The most popular pay-off lines usually consist of three short notions: fast, safe & simple. And yes, pay-off lines with an alliteration score wonderfully as well, as do new, invented words like THINNOVATION for the MacBook Air, or Travelicious for the annual travel event organized by OAD travel agency.

Take a look at your own company or brand name and try to find out if and how your customers abbreviate your name. What's your brand called in the streets, in everyday slang? The easier this name sticks in the mind and is enriched by a great three-part pay-off line, the sooner you'll reach the brain position necessary to hit the road to the heart. From IQ to EQ.

Yes indeed, the 3"12"E rule will become more crucial than ever. After all, everybody knows that GM stands for General Motors, don't they? Andy Warhol was right when he said "Everyone will be famous for 15 minutes," although he was talking about 15 minutes of worldwide fame. By now, you have to do it within 15 seconds.

Giorgio Armani

There are always protests, whether you do something **GOOD OR BAD**. Even if you do something beneficial, people say you do it because it's **ADVERTISING**

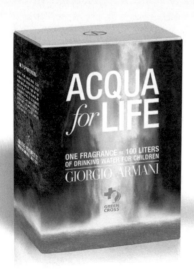

Nowadays, Every Opinion Counts, So You Better Watch Out...

Now that everything is available and clear to everyone, people tend to look for ulterior motives, even in reference to charitable and worthy causes. This is why the RED project by fashion king Armani and singer Bono, among others, was initially viewed as a way of generating more publicity for themselves, perish the thought. Whereas it was intended to fight AIDS, malaria and TB by linking well-known brand names to the good cause! This is probably the effect of the economic stagnation swamp that we find ourselves in at the moment. Almost every initiative is suspiciously scrutinized and examined. You often read justified rants about all sorts of scams on Twitter, but just as often the abuse is not at all fair and only serves to set the (aggressive) tone right away. This can happen to anybody or anything, be it the preservation of a unique and important lecture or of our artistic heritage. Everyone will first relate the subject to their own situation, consider whether it's useful to respond and then send the message out into the world.

As for that, everybody has suddenly taken on the role of journalist and is 'personally involved'. Anyone can voice an opinion, even on TV. In Europe, lots of people think the government shouldn't subsidize the poorer southern European countries that are having a rough time in the current economy, and they're not afraid to say so out loud on TV. Judging by some nations' finances, even the richer countries are having difficulty funding basic provisions, let alone artistic projects, museums and theaters. Which means that rich individuals and big companies will increasingly be asked to sponsor these projects and institutions. Because what would the Dutch be without the great Rijksmuseum? That's just as hard to imagine as the Guggenheim being closed down. Of course, it's just as important to preserve the local brass bands and theater companies. We'll just have to get used to having to contribute a bit more to arts and culture, as the government is slashing all kinds of subsidies. The new commercial truth is that everything has its price. That is why many English pubs post the slogan "In God we trust, all others pay cash." If you use it in a different sense, as in "In art we trust, the rest have to pay," you're still on shaky ground. Will the arts survive? Especially in times when survival has become an art form in itself.

Let's be a bit more optimistic and establish that there are still a lot of people willing to contribute to the creative arts. If you're one of them, then the next question is: what should or shouldn't I do? What's really cool to do, and what could turn against me? Being a sponsor is all about helping others without expecting anything in return. It goes without saying that such activities have to suit your brand and must be supported by your employees. The cause you're going to support needs to be visible to everyone, your staff should be able to 'visit' the cause, as it were, and above all, it must feel good.

Maybe, in the near future, you too will be swamped with requests for donations and financial aid. Suppose you've decided to go through these applications twice a year, then you can always tell the applicants that you're unable to respond to everything at once. Tell them the sponsorship needs to be within your budget and suitable for your company. But be careful, because these days your response may backfire. So always tell people there's a waiting list, don't raise false hopes and wait at least six business days before sending a reply. If something funny or original attracts your attention and you decide to support it, you can always call and say: "You're the exception to the rule. I've checked right away. We're going to help you...". Be sure not to commit yourself for several years to long-term projects. Always say that you review all applications yearly, since there might be some new initiatives you want to support next year. And if you actually decide to support their cause for a second year, they'll be very happy with you. As soon as they take your support for granted, they usually also forget to thank you for your troubles. If you're not ready to commit, you can always tell them that you review applications only twice a year!

Who would you like to support, to lend financial aid? It isn't always about money: above all, it's about compassion. You can also organize a fundraiser, a dinner, for example. In the Netherlands they have a big dinner on Dam square on World AIDS day. You can do it too; on the first of March or October! Find a cause you'd like to support. Invite all your customers and your own staff, charge them for the dinner and afterwards, double the proceeds from your own pocket. This will give people a taste for more, and you'll get an opportunity to meet your customers during EQ time, outside business hours.

Or does that make it too commercial?

Start Pre-Selling, It Never Fails...

If everything is as it should be with a presentation, you invest most energy in the presentation itself, but good preparation is just as important. Never give a presentation without preparing, that's absolutely not done, and you won't deserve to win. Besides, your customers (your audience) will immediately sense this, they have a second sense for it. And you know, anticipating on your customers' behavior and preparing for this can be great fun, and if you don't want to leave anything to chance, it's plain necessary. Only, try to avoid the common pitfall of looking too far ahead. It may produce some nice plans, but these are often impracticable. Think of this iron rule: "It is a mistake to look too far ahead. Only one link of the chain of destiny can be handled at a time."

In short, everything comes down to the hour in which you're allowed to present yourself or your company, or both. You're hoping to pluck the stars from the sky in those 60 minutes, and you hope your audience will choose your offer, proposal, work of art, building plan, insurance policy, or whatever. If you manage to gracefully work your way towards that moment of choice, it may result in an enormous rush of adrenaline, necessary to make the difference. If you think about it, it's a pity that your customers will never be aware of all your preparations. That's why it's important to send out the message that you're really looking forward to the presentation in question. Although you do need to be sincere, real, and above all, funny. If you somehow betray that you're afraid to lose, you've already lost the race. Winners take the initiative, losers just make up excuses to justify their loss.

Let's compare this process to two icebergs. While the summits of both icebergs appear to be miles apart, under water they're already touching. Now, imagine for a second that the visible portion of the icebergs stands for conscious action, and the submerged part stands for our unconscious mind. Well then, the trick is to try and bring the unconscious mind up to the surface of consciousness, even before the presentation begins. As we say in marketing terms: make the EQ travel to the IQ and let the 'bliss' take place beforehand. If the receiver senses everything is okay, you've won the race before it has even started.

Modern-day technology, i.e. e-mail for the older generation and WhatsApp for Generation Z, makes this fully possible. YouTube has become the world's preferred supplier of interesting videos that beg to be edited and used, and lots of TV shows do just that. But you can do this too. For instance, you could add your own subtitles to the video of Yeltsin meeting Clinton, and send the video to your audience in advance. Write something like "We're looking forward to tomorrow's meeting!", then let Clinton speak his own words, laughing like crazy, and then add this subtitle: "This will be the funniest

presentation we ever gave." If you climb the stage after such an appetizer, the 3"12" and even the E will already be yours. And in nine out of ten cases, people will be busily discussing the action you've taken beforehand, which will immediately raise the bar for your competitor, 1-0 to you.

If you aren't yet ready for such actions, and you're virtually computer illiterate, then you can also bring some old-fashioned apple pies to the meeting. Before you know it, you'll be talking about the taste of the most common pie in your youth. About peeling the apples with your mother and the wonderful smell when the pies were baking in the oven. It's all about making people realize how much effort you've put into it in order to win, how much willpower you have. The more energy people sense, the more opportunities you've created for yourself. The better the preparation, the greater the effect. Because you shouldn't be sorry afterwards and feel that you didn't do enough. Then you'll be very, very sorry, won't you?

You see, we still aren't able to travel backwards in time, but we can think ahead and that's where the profit is for the taking.

What can you do to make sure you win the race in advance? At any rate, make sure you enjoy doing it. If your prospect does not appreciate your efforts, which is always possible, then you wouldn't have enjoyed working for this customer, anyway. All the fun is incorporated in the business DNA, on the path to greater business happiness. If you're not working in the same spirit and you notice this on time, you'll save yourself a lot of future problems. So you win after all...

New Channels Are Screaming for 'Impulse' Attention...

In the last ten years, the way we search for product information and the way we shop and buy has drastically changed and evolved. Just look at the music industry or the travel business. But you ain't seen nothing yet. By the next decade, an entire generation will be used to shopping on the Internet with the help of a smartphone that will even actively help them purchase the goods. Shopping, or at least browsing, will increasingly take place online. You can buy all sorts of things with a simple mouse click.

Nevertheless, people will still gather in specific places in order to travel, to wait, to work or to engage in sports activities. Here, there will be plenty of new opportunities to attract attention and find favor with the general public. For instance, look at the evolution of the bookstore; many stores fiercely oppose the emergence of eBooks, while it would be much wiser if they embraced this trend instead. Why doesn't every book on their shelves have a QR code with which customers can immediately download the book and pay for it at the cash register? This would be particularly wonderful for customers who don't quite trust paying through the Internet. You can also think of all sorts of funny gadgets for downloading eBooks: customers could bring along their own USB sticks, but you could also sell various geeky USB sticks in the bookstore, or different kinds of cool storage devices. Or... you're in a plane and you read about a great book that rings a bell, such as *Great to Cool,* or *Everybody CEO* by Dutch innovator and strategist Menno Lanting; nothing easier than to download the book right away, is there? It makes great in-flight reading. You might even get a free eBook in KLM's business class, who knows? Railway companies could do something similar in the high-speed Thalys or ICE trains, because these are places where people stay for longer periods of time and can find the time to do 'something' with a book.

Here's another example: you're standing in line in the company

cafeteria and you can easily retrieve your favorite e-magazine while you wait, what about that? New, just released, or "hey, how nice to come across this item all of a sudden": these are all thoughts that pop up in people's minds once in a while, that attract their attention and create the desire to buy. Such attention often leads to impulse buying.

Where could you accidentally pop up and ignite the 3" spark? Always strive to enrich your basic supply with trendy and attractive impulse products that will be perceived as added value. Everybody will be glad to see these extras and in return, you will generate additional turnover, which means extra profit. Hence, a win-win situation.

> News is made by the public, and today's media follow the news! **SO CREATE NEWS,** that's the way it **WORKS**
>
> — René C.W. Boender

The 'Make-Contact Media Mix' Is On & Offline...

Although this mix will become real only when it makes the paper. Let's get back to basics for a minute: no contract without contact! Anything can establish contact if you want it to, and it's important to continually renew this contact. That provides the public with an alibi to notice you and visit your store again. We're talking about the whole package here, from the sign-board outside your store to your showcase, from your website to your activities on the social networks. The ultimate proof for this is provided time and time again: if your website looks fresh and is filled with relevant, up-to-date content, traffic to your site will increase by 5%, just like that, and the time people spend browsing on your site will increase by a staggering 20%. Put a new display in your clean shop window and people will stop to look, put a new offer on the sign-board and people will check it out (the 3" PAR).

People are spoiled for choice and have gotten used to things being updated and refreshed all the time. If you want to leave things as they are, then that's your decision. But beware of the consequences! The general public is always looking for new things and curiosity is innate. "Be the First to Know," as CNN used to say: a primal force that drives attention. And the beauty of the times we're living in is that everybody thinks of himself as a journalist and dutifully passes on the message on YouTube or Twitter. Also, the news is increasingly being supplied with content created on smartphones! Make no mistake; the content is created and read by the general public, the media merely follow the public. This means they're not in the lead, although they're essential in the newsmaking business.

The boomerang from online to offline and back again will get things going. But it will only come to life and connect with the masses once the classic media, that is, newspapers and TV or radio, pick up your message and lend it classic wings. Newspapers are even better at it than television, which always remains a bit of a superficial medium. Although television producers have noticed this and are aware of the fact that just producing TV content is no longer sufficient. Of course, they still get excited when their show manages to attract 1 million viewers more than the previous edition, even Ryan Seacrest will be happy with such a result. Except for John de Mol, perhaps, since his *The Voice* shows habitually have a TV rating of more than 11 million viewers in the US. By the way, do you know how these ratings work? Don't be surprised, the TV ratings are mostly researched by a company called Nielsen, and are based on the preferences of about 5,000 households nationwide that are considered representative for the US. Oh yes, 5,000 households that either decide to watch or not to watch, can make or break the future of TV shows and producers, and in so doing influence what's headline news. Or should we say: used to decide and used to influence?

you see, the TV ratings will soon start sliding downhill even faster than the dollar or the euro, because in future what matters will be the topics that are discussed in public. And these will be determined by 'likes', Twitter messages and all kinds of online TV shows. People say: "Links become likes." Now don't stop reading, here's the explanation: likes are a kind of rating that people can give to express their satisfaction regarding a certain product or website. Often, you can indicate you like something by clicking the relevant 'thumbs up' icon on a web page. Obviously, a large number of likes regarding a specific website will influence the surfing and buying behavior of the Internet crowd.

As a result of the new working hours we'll be watching TV when it suits us, as Generation Z already does; this will further diminish the importance of TV ratings. At least, they won't be as relevant as before. And more apps such as 'Trendrr' will emerge, which companies and brands can use to monitor their popularity and media coverage. Then the real figures will surface, and with it, the truth about brand recognition and relevance. So don't be fooled by the TV ratings, but also consider the other factors that play a part in this circus. For instance, lots of noise on the social websites about a certain show is more influential than the cold figures that are registered at the time the show was broadcast. It's important to know this, because it will help you decide when to air your commercial on TV.

What's that, you're not on TV? Then think about the number of fresh signals you've sent out in order to claim attention, whether it's through your sign-board or your shop window. And don't forget your website, which includes a lively blog, of course, with relevant content.

Go have a look right now, is everything fresh and tempting enough?

The Rules of Impact Still Apply...

If you do something, do it right; good won't do, you need to make it great. If you get a kick out of it, someone else will probably also get excited by it. In short: cool is the new hot. But...how can you make it so hot that everyone would love to take a look at it? Creating is a craft, a specialism that is practiced by extremely talented people with lots of expertise, people who love to reach others, and know how to affect them. Especially in these complicated times, with all the possibilities offered by the social media, you need talented people who can help you with your publicity and marketing. Naturally, there are quite a few entrepreneurs who manage to perform these tasks themselves, and not without success, but it's very difficult to keep making an impact using the DIY method.

That's why it's a good idea to cooperate with agencies or people who know how it works and are able to secure a brain position for you. Remember that buying or deserving attention is no small feat, don't underestimate this craft. Then again, advertising agencies and marketing companies need to realize that their customers might have some ideas of their own that are worthwhile; they would be wise not to completely discard these proposals, but to try to work them in. For instance, KLM Airlines' Tile & Inspire concept, which invites Facebook fans and other customers to create their own Delft blue porcelain tile, decorated with their profile photo and their own slogan. Such an idea comes straight from the customer's soul. Therefore, you should always try to embrace good concepts and attempt to make them even better than they are.

It's better to spend a bit more on the impact of your idea, then to cut costs by eliminating the agency or your own creative group.

The media (including the social media) require the biggest investment. You simply have to spend time and money on these. If you really want to do it all by yourself, but have no idea where to start, then you could use this old Hollywood rule: make it big and use white lettering on a red background. Just like *The Economist*, which sports a large red logo on the cover. Guaranteed to work. Or let monkeys do the talking, as you can see on YouTube, guaranteed to attract hits. Then again, you can always let 'it', whatever it may be, explode with lots of noise, a true bang for attention. Although it's better to take your time and create the impact that will make people roll on the floor with laughter. That will make you stand out, just as much as a blond in a red dress.

Can you remember when you last flung such a message into the world? And what will be your next message? Your audience, your staff, your customers, but your family too, they all deserve it, so do your job and begin with a smile. They will feel and see this in each sentence, in each advertising slogan, and that's how you'll break through the code.

Privacy Is Becoming Piracy, So Start Managing It...

Lots of things have become better and easier because of the new ICT revolution, but unfortunately the new apps don't solve all problems. By now, the only thing that remains truly private is what's in your head that you've not told anyone yet. The rest is public property, like it or not. Along with the ICT revolution we are now witnessing a new type of piracy not instigated by Big Brother or the government, but rather by malicious individuals who can actually destroy you in the online world. Dutch trendwatcher Adjiedj Bakas revealed some of these practices in his book *The End of Privacy*.

In the old days you had to deal with gossip and scandal, all by word of mouth. Then came the tabloids and all sorts of gossip magazines that earned money selling gossip. Since rumors usually turned into old news after a few weeks and the magazines had already been recycled by then, this was usually literally the end of the story. Alas, this is no longer the case, at present everything and anything is saved on the Internet, thanks to Facebook, Twitter, LinkedIn, and all the other websites that store many terabytes of private information on the net. Every great and wonderful thing is saved forever, but so are some things you'd prefer to forget and delete at once. A nice spring-cleaning of the Internet would not be a bad idea, send all the rubbish on a one-way trip to the graveyard, so you wouldn't need to face the same nonsensical and offensive messages over and over again.

Marketing expert Seth Godin wrote on the subject, arguing that there are people who don't know your work, haven't taken the time to understand your point of view, and yet feel the need to express an opinion about you and what you do. For example, 'I don't like Angelina Jolie.' 'Which movie didn't you like?' 'Oh, I've never seen any of her movies. I just don't like her.' On the more positive side, celebrity, and particularly social media celebrity (which more and more of us have every day) earns you trust, access and an audience. Your Twitter followers or friends of friends on Facebook are more likely to cut you some slack because you're not a stranger. But it's unreasonable to expect only the upside, Godin says. There are simply people in the world "who don't know you and who don't like you."

Companies, artists, but maybe you too, as a private individual, have to deal with the new reality that springs from all this. At least, until we've invented filters that can keep this stuff away from us; until then we'll need to play an active part in managing the Internet. Web care will become a prerequisite and some excellent web care agencies will emerge that will be happy to perform this task for you. You see, it also works the other way round, you can also let the positive messages trickle through the net. The dark side of this new reality is, that you can find someone in the Ukraine or India, and pay them 200 or 300 dollars to make life so difficult for your competitor, an artist, or your ex-wife, that their reputation is completely destroyed. At first this will only affect you online, but before you know it, you'll be finished in the offline world too.

Let's conclude that it is much better to prepare for these situations than to be forced to react at a later stage, when it might be too late. Anyhow, bankers have become much better at fighting 'phishing', that is fishing for private information on bank customers. The tsunami of Internet fraud will be one of our biggest headaches for some years to come. Pirates who steal your web identity and pretend to be you, while you have nothing to do with the whole thing.

How is the state of affairs in your business? In private and in company life? Make sure you give your undivided attention to this phenomenon, it's an absolute priority. Before you know it, someone is blurting all kinds of 'live' nonsense, fueled by 'evil'.

Put Pen to Paper...

What's the worst that can happen to you? That's easy: no Internet, which means everything will come to a standstill. As a result of a power outage, for example, or because your own mobile network is down. Immediately after Apple's Steve Jobs died in October 2011, and just before the iPhone 4S came onto the market, BlackBerry experienced the biggest power failure ever in their network. Almost at once, the whole world started joking that this had to be Steve's work; he had arrived in heaven and was eager to try out the tiny buttons on the device he so loathed when he was still alive, and as a result, BB went down. Then Moses interfered and the problem was solved, because he forbade Steve to tinker with BlackBerry any longer! Could it be true, is there more between heaven and earth?

Anyhow, we can safely conclude that here on Earth, everything comes to a standstill without electricity. We've become addicted to electric current and we hardly know what to do without power. We're used to it and spoiled by it. If you want to have some fun, just watch the 'Broken escalator' video on YouTube: http://www.youtube.com/watch?v=47rQkTPWW2I. And show this video

to your colleagues, in particular; then they can marvel at people who spend the night on an escalator that refuses to roll on, instead of simply using their legs to climb upstairs. Life stops without current, can this really be true? Even if it were so, there's a very easy way to keep in touch with others, it's nice and original. Not just for Christmas but also for no reason at all, out of the blue. What about this? Put pen to paper for a change, write a letter by hand, in your best handwriting.

Can you still remember the last handwritten letter you received, or a thank-you note with a personal message? You may count yourself lucky if that last note was from your father or mother. For example, if it was your mother's favorite chicken soup recipe, because you wanted to make this soup too, for the first time in your life? Cherish that letter and save it forever, so Mom's chicken soup will taste even better every time you make it. But it's also a great way to distinguish yourself in business, you could say it creates business happiness much quicker. Together with a market researcher I tested this, by sending out 2 x 100 letters. The first 100 recipients received a neatly typed letter; the second group of 100 recipients got a handwritten letter from the CEO. The content was exactly the same as the typewritten letter, but it had a personal touch. The result: the handwritten letter got twice as many replies!

To be able to communicate in a successful and sympathetic way under all circumstances, be it in business or in private life, you need to possess wisdom and creativity. It's wise not to deal with certain matters through a cold e-mail message or a typed letter, but to take the time to write a message by hand.

Who are you going to write in the true sense? Do it, it's fun; it may cost a bit more time, but it's definitely worth the trouble. Even flowers become much prettier if you add a handwritten, personal message on the card. Don't hesitate, start writing, because you will address your own happiness, as it were, and it gives you a chance to use all your talents again. Because all business happens to be personal business.

I've **GOT THE BRAIN** of a four year old. I'll bet he was glad to be **RID OF IT**

Groucho Marx

Headache, Migraine, or a Positive Brain Position...

What happens inside the customer's head when he thinks about you? Does this thought trigger a positive wave or a tsunami of negative feelings? What kind of thoughts sprout in the customer's brain, without you having talked to him personally? Do your clients develop a headache when they merely think of a meeting with you folks, do they leave the meeting with an awful migraine? It's mostly the consultants who first identify this problem, as they are in the front line of customer care. Unfortunately, their visit to the customer seldom solves the problem and sometimes even worsens it. In the end you're crying out for help, and wondering who can help you out of this misery.

Don't despair, because there is a solution; you see, establishing contact as described above is a thing of the past. The first thing you need to do is to find people who can help you tackle your problems, and will go through hell for you, in a positive way. You will find those people, don't worry. It isn't that hard to get the hang of this positive attitude, you need to adopt it as a starting point in everything you do, even if things go against you for a while. You can economize on lots of things, except on genuine commitment and you're equipped with a wide range of natural skills to show this commitment. Do whatever you do best and try to make it even better. Not through a cold, hardnosed e-mail message, but in a real meeting, eye to eye, an encounter. Look each other in the eye and make sure it's fun to be together. This sounds a bit obvious, but in this day and age, it's especially these moments that are economized.

Now don't you think that sending an e-mail means you've made contact, no, you should actually try to meet in person, in the same room. Discuss the past as little as you can, concentrate on the future. The 'invisible belief' which is future-oriented will provide an energetic lift off, as various social-psychological studies have shown. It's worthwhile to read a book on this subject. A whole new world will open up to you and it won't give you a headache. You will gain authority and, above all, you will get the customer's sympathy! It all begins with you. You need to say something that makes sense, good content makes all the difference. If you're just producing a lot of noise you'll never get the right brain position and you'll leave your customer behind with a bad migraine. But if you manage to make the difference, then you've got your man.

To be on the safe side, always bring some aspirin, this way you will always have a remedy at hand, in case the meeting goes sour. At least, they will realize you've got a sense of humor. If you come across as an inspired, passionate and committed person, you will have attained the position of the bliss. You will automatically pop up in someone's right brain half when they have a need for your product or service.

What can you do to reach that point? Honestly, it isn't as hard as you think...

The Inflation of 'Like & Endorse Me'...

In future, **Human Resources departments will have an easier time than ever.** And at the same time, they will be facing serious difficulties. The challenge they face is how to separate the chaff from the wheat, how to recognize true quality. What is true and what is rubbish? Nowadays, the Internet bears witness to a lot of lies and fantasies! If you think about it, it's become quite easy to screen job applicants in a matter of moments: just look them up on Google and you will have all the facts of their lives handed to you on a platter. And why not also do a quick check on Facebook? We're all very careless in using this medium, so you'll get an impression of what someone is like right away. Then skip to LinkedIn for a moment and you can view their networks. There is just one 'but': watch out for the pitfall of the 'Like' and 'Endorse me' utterances. At the moment, every social network site offers the possibility to judge and rate others, or be judged or rated by others.

How often have you been asked to do this by an acquaintance or business relation? And how often did you stick to the truth, and only the truth, while sending in your reference? Did you actually write down the thoughts that entered your mind when somebody asked you for one? Possibly you did not know exactly what to write and you did so with a heavy heart. Usually, these requests come from people who are looking for another job, who are busy creating their own legend, as it were, and don't hesitate to use the whole universe to achieve their goal. The 'wow' in mere seconds, because the 3"12"E rule applies there, too. Although in this area, you can see inflation creeping in, the value of these references is decreasing. Often, you are so fond of a certain Facebooker who asks you for a positive review, that you click the 'thumbs up' icon within a nanosecond. At LinkedIn you reflect a while longer, and then write a brief and to-the-point reference in beautiful English, in praise of the person you want to support. You tend to exaggerate and write "he will always keep challenging the status quo and has a keen eye for things that remain invisible to others", or: "This woman is a CFO where the F stands for fun to work with". Every once in a while, you know better... Actually, you'd like to write she's a bookkeeping, money-grabbing miser, but that you always try to stay friends because at least she pays her bills on time! That would be true honesty, wouldn't it?

Most 'likes' are given out of compassion, out of the desire not to disappoint the other person. A growing number of people read these references with a kind of advertising filter in their head, they take them with a pinch of salt. Here you will find out that it actually can hurt you if you attribute certain skills or merits to someone and don't stick to the truth. In any case, this definitely goes for negative comments, but if your reference is way too positive, this rule applies as well. The reader who consults such a profile will perceive you as an unreliable person. This goes to show that top of person awareness (TOPA) is important. Who is the person claiming this fact? And above all, who are you, the transmitter of such messages? You are a brand, that's why you will need to stick to your image as a brand and truthfully tell the world what you think of something or someone.

'Welcome to the Relationship Era', because it's all about relationships. The brand relationship too, let's call it the TOBA relationship your brand fosters with others. Say goodbye to the old rule that it's all about positioning, preemption and unique selling position! Nowadays it's all about the ISP: the inspirational selling point.

You can safely delete everything you thought you knew, you can land with both feet firmly on the ground again, face up towards heaven. The most important thing is the love of the people. For a brand, that is.

Look around and write down some sentences; what feels right? Just for fun, type 'I love Apple' on your computer, or 'I love Starbucks'. Lovemarks have the SQ, which is given and expressed by real people. This is the difference between buying and being bought. Pay attention to this when you decide to 'like' or endorse someone; before you announce your love for a certain person, you need to be sure you sincerely mean it. The public does exactly the same thing when it comes to the love of a specific brand. Stop the 'like' inflation, begin introducing honesty, even if you sometimes have trouble saying what you really think.

Telling the truth in a friendly manner is more than OK.

Customers Have a Sixth Sense, and a Network.

One of the most essential issues in the world of business is how you deal with your customers' complaints. Recently, Dutch comedian Youp van 't Hek attracted mass attention to this subject by starting a Twitter campaign aimed at the failing customer service of telecom provider T-Mobile. Before you knew it, it no longer mattered whether he was right or wrong. Everything revolved around the commotion he managed to stir up. If you adequately handle these complaints, you will be praised and forgiven; if you don't you will be SM'd! In other words: punished in the social media, in such a way that it will keep hounding you. In public, and often in a way that is not very decent or commendable. It speaks for itself that it has become very easy to inflict such punishments, since consumers all have the weapon of using the social media at their disposal. And they're not afraid to use and deploy this weapon.

Customers have a sixth sense for noticing whether they've been taken for a ride, or have been kept dangling. So don't do this, don't play games with your customers' emotions, be glad they have taken the trouble to call you. Most professional service providers who use a call center are fully aware of this. The *Big Nothing* shows this very clearly and paints a picture of the very special way of life in a call center. Watch http://www.youtube.com/watch?v=hAjzvy94JsM, but don't follow this example. Please, don't do it this way, before you know it you will get the boomerang back through the social media and it will cost you more than you can gain in the short run. Curious? Well okay, here's a clue: the video shows a very crowded call center with employees who are all sweet and sugary when they deal with customers on the phone, but blow off steam in between calls, by abusing the customers, albeit in a very funny way.

By the way, the best call center employees you can get, in search of the highest Consumer Satisfaction Index, are people who are disabled in some way or other. Visually impaired call center employees pick up more than employees who have vision, and even people with no arms or legs move around easier in such an environment than we do. Without having the use of arms and legs, Nick Vujicic has become one of the world's top motivational speakers. Since he was born this way, he doesn't know any better, but his golf shot is better than yours! During his keynote talk you will choke with laughter. Wow, so this is how you can do it too! Why don't you pay a virtual visit to www.lifewithoutlimbs.org? Wouldn't you love to have him work for your company? Wouldn't he be an asset and have a worthwhile contribution to make?

If this is so, why don't you employ more people with a disability? How is your company doing in this respect? Why don't you ask your call center about this? If you use a call center, that is. Those of us who must live our lives differently also unleash a different way of thinking with regard to all sorts of current problems. Remember: in this day and age, call centers aren't an unnecessary, costly expense for a company, but rather an investment in customer loyalty! And we consumers should have some more respect while communicating with them, since getting mad will get us nowhere. Simply explain your problem and stay calm, that's a better idea. As long as you stay within reason, you will usually be presented with a solution to your problems.

We Live Longer but We Stay Younger

In the past 100 years, life expectancy in the Western world has been prolonged by 25 years on average. Very nice, but it also brings a lot of physical discomfort. Great to have an extra 25 years, unless you're ill and suffering all kinds of ailments. This can be avoided if we manage to change course, drastically change our eating habits, and start exercising and living differently, of course. A scientific study recently discovered that it is wise to eat just a little bit less than you would like to. We're talking about a reliable source here, not some diet guru who claims this.

If you eat a little less than you're used to, your body will react by burning everything that's available; then it will activate the 'helpdesk' in its brain, which will cause the body to use more energy for repairing the DNA structure, instead of converting this energy to growth (that is to say: fat). Source: Erasmus University, Rotterdam.

In other words, if you accustom yourself from the age of twenty to eat and 'graze' a bit less than you'd like to, you might live pleasantly for about 20 to 25 years longer. The age of retirement could easily be pushed forward to 67 or even 70, no problem. Because you know you will have enough time left to enjoy all the other things in life, and in the world. It will also provide you with more opportunities to hire senior employees and make use of their vast experience. And don't make the same mistake as some TV critics who think CBS anchor man Charlie Rose is too old and only fit for senior citizens' TV networks.

By the way, how old is your crew? Take into account that the average age of your employees will increase in future, and start preparing for this. Also, take the study mentioned above to heart, because there is so much else you can enjoy aside from things related to business happiness. For example, have a nice life, and dream of getting older while you're still young. Only, don't postpone everything to the point of retirement, don't forget to live day by day and enjoy it. Time is relative and it's all over before you know it…

True Leaders Are Vulnerable and Have Guts …

Nobody will benefit from you panicking, actually: panic spreads quickly and before you know it the most awful things happen. Especially in this age of Twitter, since panic can easily be summarized within the 144 characters available for your tweet. In these exceptional circumstances, women tend to talk and start twittering without thinking first, and men tend to do the opposite, to spring into action without using their brains. The second option is worse, and can cause accidents instead of inspiring people.

That is why a leader always needs to represent hope, and be optimistic but also realistic in his choice of words and communication; this creates confidence. A leader needs to be a visionary who wants to share his vision of the future with his followers, no matter who he is, Obama or Sarkozy. Although the same applies to you as a leader of your project, company, or country. If you're not sure about the direction you want to take, you will have lost before you've begun, and that makes you a bad leader. The path you take is the path you choose, the moment you hesitate is the moment you lose. If you have a choice between two tracks, then don't always take the easy and predictable way out, but choose the hardest route! You might experience some friction, but this route will undoubtedly be less crowded, while the easiest route is usually overcrowded. Feasible but difficult works better than achieving something without making any effort; since if it were this easy, everyone would do it this way.

Acting is important, guts is important and sometimes requires a bit of extra force and some strong language. Apart from the art of Just Fucking Do It (JFDI), there is also the art of not doing anything. The art of letting unimportant things be, which means you don't need to feel compelled to take any action. You might be able to remember a whole lot, but are you also wise enough to forget? Always keep in mind that it's about the bigger picture, not about insignificant details that can bog you down. Don't fuss over trivialities, don't be sorry about what you have done, but rather about the things you haven't done, because that's what people will judge you for. Only those that don't understand become angry, those who understand are wise, to quote an ancient Indian saying.

Above all, don't forget to adopt a vulnerable position. Nobody is omniscient and it will only foster confidence if you admit to not knowing something once in a while. Now you have read about all the demands you need to fulfill as a leader, you may realize that taking the 'hot' step from great to cool might be more difficult than you thought, although it is essential in order to grab the ISP, the Inspirational Selling Point. What matters is the feeling that your internal and external customers get when they see you and your product, and reliable leadership will enhance this feeling.

Always work with optimists, if you can, since optimism generates more energy; even if you've already been damaged, it is better to die with a smile on your face than waste away crying in a corner. Think about this: whatever business you have, it's all just a game. That is why you should carefully select the partners with who you do business, and try to work for and with optimists. Because an optimist laughs to forget, but a pessimist forgets to laugh. That is a very good reason to refer pessimists to the background, since you are just one of many options to them. Really, it is all up to you...not up to them. He who represents hope, owns the future!

Be the most ambitious dealer in this, and anyone will trust and follow you.

Break Through the Routine, the Grind, and the Fixed Patterns

It has been said before: every attempt you don't make, is bound to fail. Always get your energy from the present, the here and now; you are allowed to look backwards for a moment, but not for very long. You need to focus on the future and not on the past. Prosperity despite resistance is something you can create yourself, nobody else will do it for you. You don't even need to have a lot of money to break through the routine; the intention to do it is much more important. At this thought, many develop a lower back pain or start hyperventilating, since it appears that you will have to get up from the couch and try to get others to move, too. Because couch potatoes and safety seekers have a vested interest in bleak grey colors and tend not to change anything in a hurry. Even so, you will need to tear down the fixed patterns that have entered all of our lives, by force if necessary, but preferably by a motivating attitude that broadens the mind.

This doesn't mean you have to resort to narcotics; just send your staff outside for a day, into the world. Let them look around at some other company and get some inspiration. Changing places for a day works miracles and provides a breath of fresh air, and above all, a new take on the future. Especially if you return to the work floor, if you are a manager or director. Managers and executives have often long forgotten what the actual problems are in the workplace. And the other way round, employees can also be mistaken in judging the dilemmas executives have to face. Looking at things from a different perspective will help solve problems quickly, and will influence the atmosphere positively. It will provide fresh input in the company. While you are at it, why don't you ask what the 'outside world' thinks of your company. Then you'll quickly find out that you can change negative tendencies around with a little effort from everyone involved.

Keep asking questions and organize an open discussion day for your crew. Just make up an issue that may seem a bit far-fetched, something you can hardly imagine. Today's reality is that 'too big to fail' doesn't exist anymore; any company may get into trouble at a given moment. For example, you are manufacturing a product in which a large amount of plastic is processed, and suddenly the supply of this raw material runs out. This is not entirely fictitious, since you need crude oil to manufacture plastic, and oil is running out. What would you do in such a case? Try to squeeze the last drops of oil from every nook and cranny? Fight against nature? Yes, of course you could take that course. Or, you could let your best people work out a solution, invent an alternative material which is even easier to mold and manipulate than plastic.

Here's another example: as an electronics manufacturer you are increasingly faced with a shortage of natural energy sources, and because your equipment uses lots of electricity you will need to come up with a solution, and fast. Develop devices that use solar power, wind or water, or maybe some different source of energy altogether, something that's not so obvious. Or you can decide to devote your own time and energy to inventing energy-saving products.

You better believe that a whole new set of rules applies the minute your feet get wet or too hot, in such a case the game is played in a different way. But why wait for this? Start to act right away and it will give you an advantage over your competitor. Because chances are that they are actually waiting to get wet. Come on; the rules haven't been invented to be maintained for all eternity, they are screaming to be rewritten. So how about it...

FAST IS FINE, but accuracy is EVERYTHING

— Wyatt Earp

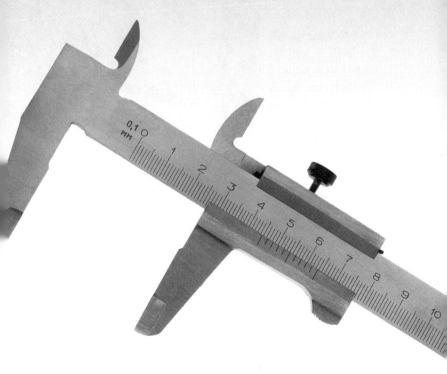

More Speed, Service & Fun...

E very once in a while you need to take a moment to reflect, only to come to the conclusion that speed is the best engine to accomplish change, in your turnaround from cool to hot. To make sure you're going to claim a better brain position in future. It's the same in sports: before FC Barcelona enters the arena you are already seated in your favorite chair, full of anticipation, because your inner voice tells you this is going to be great! Nowadays, the players' speed and technical skills are so magnificent that it's a pleasure to watch, in slow motion too. Barcelona are the best, of course, with soccer players like Xavi and Messi the genius. And even at the dentist's, speed is everything;

the drill is so fast that you don't even notice it and the cavity is filled before you have the time to feel anything. The sense of speed gives you a pleasant buzz.

Likewise, the newest and most successful Apps have everything to do with speed and fun. Take a look at the Dutch communication app Scan2Chat, for instance. An opportunity to quickly find soul mates in your own neighborhood, without wasting time searching. It's smooth and efficient. As you know, being able to communicate at lightning speed is the key to success, according to the 3"12"E rule. That is to say, it will increase the chance of becoming more successful than you've been until now. Can you manage to provide your customers with all sorts of service using fewer clicks than your competitor? Do you have it in you to motivate your repairs crew in such a way that they can fix a car 20% faster than your rival, and keep surprising the client time after time with their speed and service? Will your employees work their hearts out to the tune of their cheerful whistles? And finally, could you motivate the back office to do their work so efficiently and punctually that it becomes a joy for the front office to tell the customer everything is done, while the customer still thinks it's going to take days to fix things?

As soon as you discover that it's fun to provide good service and if you truly believe in this principle, you will be rewarded much more quickly and generously by your customers. Turn this into a sport, and make sure you go into training to accomplish this. If you can do it quicker, then do it. Gunslingers like Wyatt Earp don't exist any longer, and speed in shooting has been replaced by speed skating. And the skaters keep going faster all the time too. Take the old 1,000 meter speed skating world record for women, for instance. This was recently broken by Canadian skater Christine Nesbitt, who was more than half a second faster. Until then, everybody thought this was impossible!

The conclusion is that it seems logical and feasible for you to achieve these things as well. Every second counts...

Will You Become a Storyteller Too?

This is the honest truth: **the story you tell is the product you sell!** You always sell a story, and a good story is repeated to others. It energizes and enthuses people. Folks start listening to you and this triggers everything else. The starting point is to tell an interesting story, in which you are genuinely interested yourself, and which you are prepared to share. So don't read out a dull PowerPoint presentation, but tell a story, just as you do at home when you go tuck in your kids. Be sure to catch your audience's attention and make it exciting from the very first minute, because if you can attract attention right away, you're safe. Also, you need to dare to tell a lot, and to try to talk in a way that people can visualize your story. Use metaphors and gripping examples. Don't hold back, tell everything, give away some secrets, and be honest about the things that can go wrong. In short: no smoke and mirrors, no smoke screens and idle talk. Be sincere and truly speak from the heart, that's what attracts the public.

Moreover, always connect with your audience and keep looking them in the eye, no matter if your audience consists of 12, 120, or even 1,200 people. It's probably much easier than you've always thought. This is the trick: learn to speak the same way you usually talk. Practice this, until you can give a speech without having to refer to your notes. Or to the autocue, which seems to be indispensable to some TV anchormen and women, nowadays. Critics of this system do have a point; it's better not to have to listen to preprogrammed autoblabla. Unless you need to talk about figures and statistics. You simply cannot afford to make mistakes with these data, so always put them on paper, as a reminder. A speech is an important means of communication, so make your own story funny, and above all, human. If your audience's response is lukewarm, your speech is not good enough. You see, it needs to be great, that's when people start to think you're cool, or, hot, if you prefer.

When you listen to a truly great speaker, you're totally submerged in their inspired stories, as I wrote earlier when I was telling you about the inspiring TED website. Over the years, crowds and crowds of people have enjoyed speeches by Steve Jobs, which is why I'd like to point you to a site containing the 10 best speeches by Steve: http://thenextweb.com/apple/2011/08/25/our-top-10-most-unforgettable-steve-jobs-video-moments/. Take a good look and think about what you could do to awaken the Steve in yourself. Is it hard for you to apply the tips above, and do you think this brain candy is not for you? OK, then there's just 'one more thing', as Steve used to say. From now on, don't do it yourself any longer, let somebody else deliver the keynote talk. With love, then you'll make the step from Great to Cool in a minute. That's genuine leadership for you: be aware of your skills and your limitations, of your strong and weak points.

What are you going to do in future, what's your decision? If you don't like to stand in the limelight or on stage yourself, put your text on paper, send a blazing memo and lend wings to your story. Be bold and imaginative, write it in such a way that your crew can hear your voice in their ears, as it were. And even hear you sigh when you pause for breath...

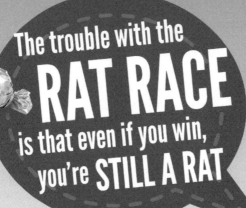

Don't Start to Work Harder when the Going Gets Hot...

There are a lot of misunderstandings regarding what to do when things start to heat up, or when it's getting way too busy around you. That is, when your company is heading in the wrong direction, or when the outside world has decided to take a shot at you. One important rule is: don't react by working even harder, but keep your distance for a while. Unless you're a firefighter, of course, and the fire is blazing all around you. Or if you're a doctor who wants to push on because it may save lives. But in all other cases, where it's 'just' about work, it is better to stand back for a moment and take a break.

For example, if you make a living in real estate, then now is the time to make the switch; from now on, thinking 'outside the box' will become thinking 'outside the blocks'. How can you find a new, useful destination for your premises? You've already noticed that persevering in doing the same thing for the same crowd doesn't really work. Here's another, very topical example: if you are in the business of organizing luxury cruise holidays, your captain may have made the mistake of waving goodbye to a friend off the Tuscany shore, and you might see your whole business go down the drain. One minute you were still thinking in terms of growth, the next you need to account for a 25% decline in turnover! Something's got to give, that's clear.

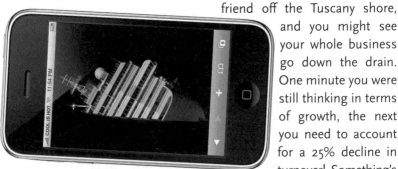

Once you're in the water, it doesn't matter how deep it is. You need to keep swimming to stay afloat; if you do nothing you will drown, no doubt about that. That shows you how things can change.

The truth is, the only essential thing in life is a stable home, a place to live and sleep, and especially a good mattress. The eight hours we spend in our beds are the most important ones. You could also go meditate, but we Westerners think this is too vague, which is a pity. Believe me, by relaxing and taking a break you can put things in perspective again. If you keep pressing on, you'll burn out, get irritated and impatient. You'll find others increasingly annoying, because tiredness and exhaustion wreck your life more than you suspect. The next morning your opinions are a bit more balanced, yet still crystal clear, unambiguous and sharp, but you'll be able to make your point much more effectively. The better rested you are, the more fluently your new initiatives come flowing from your mouth.

Many people say: seeing is believing, but why don't you turn it around; believing is seeing. So, be perfectly clear about your views on the future and share them with your audience. Even if you decide not to take action, you should announce this, let everyone know what you're planning to do. Knowing you better means loving you more, as Facebook has proven time after time. You'll notice that the discussion carries on no matter what, even if you have postponed your decision. If in your heart you know you should take action, even if it's hard, then do it anyway. As Warren Buffet once said: "I wish I was who I was when I wished that I was who I am now!" It's a joy to be able to learn from the ongoing insights from someone like Buffet. His quotes tell you where you stand in a matter of minutes.

By the way, how's your own rat race going? Most people simply hate rats, and most animals too. Except for the rattlesnake, but that's not your favorite animal either. Don't race too fast, keep your distance! And don't forget to check your mattress. Replacing the old one might be the best short-term investment ever. For now it's goodnight and good luck. Make sure you get up in a winning mood.

What to Do when the SM Have Turned Against You?

Social media have a tendency to be just like the weather, they're just as fickle. What to do when it storms or the rain comes pouring down on your head? You can't talk your way out of it, because you can't command the weather like an army. You'll need to adjust to it and cope with it. It's exactly the same with the social networks. Being celebrated is wonderful, of course, but criticism hurts and is awful. Without you having anything to do with it, you can find yourself in the middle of a discussion that you don't want to be part of. Even so, it can just happen to you, and you'll find that the responses in the social media arena are rather unpredictable. Some will applaud you and think you are right, while others will force the issue by expressing even stronger opinions. They often state their case in a very black and white way, so that all nuance is lost. If such a message that started out as a simple tweet ends up in the press, the newspapers or even on television, your goose is cooked. People tend to hear no more than the 'tweet' word and then they can't be stopped, they simply need to put in their two cents.

So, what is the best way of handling these matters? What to do? The best tactics are those of an Asian martial arts fighter. Asians don't make frontal attacks right away, but they give way first, they soften the blows by moving along with them, which hurts a lot less. Good boxers do the same thing, just watch Mohammed Ali in his prime. The rule is: learn to deal with the blows first, be flexible and go with the blow. But make sure you always remain honest and keep repeating the same principles, don't try to wriggle out of the argument. Just make sure you keep saying the same thing in other, carefully chosen words. Words that are worth repeating, or even printing as newspaper headlines or text messages. Never let others attribute to you what you didn't say. Choose your own words; that is why you should always be strict and firm and be correctly dressed (although there's no need to wear SM leather outfits, that's the wrong kind of uniform). Make sure you choose the clothes that suit you and make you feel comfortable. A tie? No tie? Jeans or maybe even a bikini? It doesn't matter, dress how you want, but stay true to your personality and be honest.

Do you remember what Clinton said at the time? "I did not have sexual relations with that woman." I believe Clinton's words were accurate, strictly in the factual sense, but were they also true? One's perception will always come true, so always try to influence people's perception if you want to change things. And what if you can't take it any longer and the storm does not abate? That's the moment you need to engage in Bedouin management: lie down on the ground and wait until the storm has passed. That's what they do, down there in the desert, since it's the only way not to get sandblasted during a desert storm; lay flat on the ground and keep your head down. If you're really trendy you call this Planking, which makes you cool again and scores you points with the Internet generation.

The essence of the story is this: no matter how hard the wind blows, every storm will blow over eventually. At the market, the fish is wrapped up in yesterday's newspaper, and nobody remembers what's in old papers. After the storm has ended you can get up again and start quietly spreading the message once more. Radiate light again, that will enlighten the mind. Once again, walking in the rain will become pleasant and the wind will give you an excuse to play with your Senz storm umbrella. Don't get stuck in the blizzard but walk towards your new challenge. If you stand still, you'll be trapped in the eye of the storm; if you keep moving you can create a whole new playground. It's up to you how big this new playground is going to be, and it's absolutely not up to those who try to limit and confine you through the social networks.

Always walk towards the light, preferably towards the sun. Before you know it, the sun will shine on you again...

Copyright and the Author's Rights...

What is true and what is not, what is mine and what used to be mine? The copyright always belongs to the author, but nowadays it's hard to find justice as an author. It has become very hard to enforce intellectual property rights in a world where multiplying and sharing have taken on a whole new meaning! At first, all we needed to do is watch out for the Chinese, because they have a totally different conception of the word 'copyright' out there: they prefer to see it as a 'right to copy'! But by now everyone and anyone copies until they're blue in the face, and even the big well-known brands do it.

These tendencies are reinforced by the influence of the Internet on a society that is chock-full of questions and insecurities, wherever you look. Wikileaks demonstrated that any system can be hacked, be it the Pentagon or the Visa credit card company. What if these hackers decided to target your company? You would be in a lot of trouble, because you wouldn't be able to defend yourself effectively. At least, not for a while. At the moment even personal Twitter and Facebook identities are being stolen, just take a look on the Twitter website. Is it actually you who is being quoted there, or someone who pretends to be you? After politicians and lawyers have been targeted in this way, Dutch lawyer Bénédicte Ficq has recently drafted a bill of law to prevent identity theft, at least in the Netherlands.

Stealing someone's identity is bad, but leaking confidential information is just as bad. With regard to the Internet, now is the time to start a worldwide debate about the meaning of copyright and whether we're entitled to the information provided by Wikileaks! On the one hand, these issues require a global government that has the authority to set the rules for the worldwide community, but on the other hand this is pretty scary and very risky. In fact, what does our government know about us? And what does Mark Zuckerberg, founder of Facebook, know about us and our affairs?

Before the SOPA (Stop Online Piracy Act) is enforced, lots of things will happen.

For now, the best we can do is not go along with the trend to spread and forward confidential information with impunity, no matter who it may concern. Don't forget, it may happen to each and every one of us; waking up on a bad day and discovering that our private information is out in the open. Let's develop a few principles together, in order to put a stop to this kind of injustice, once and for all.

A nyhow, make a start in your own life and company and set rules to counter these practices. Not by dictating things from above, that won't work; rather by agreeing to a certain code of conduct, a declaration of intent. Because where there's intent, in nine out of ten cases there also is a solution.

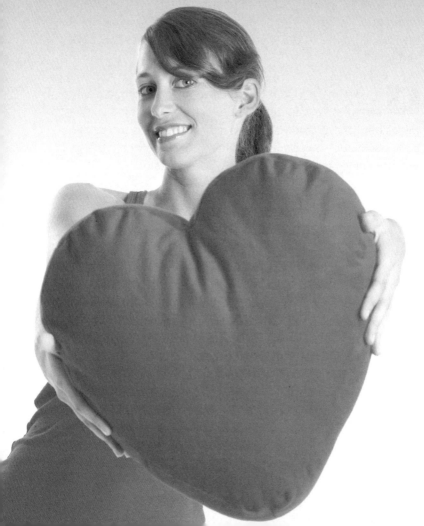

The True Meaning of Heart…

Authenticity and sincerity, these will always be the core values of anything you do, no matter what line of business you're in. It's quite easy to urge people to put their heart into something. But what matters is whether you actually do it yourself, instead of just paying lip service to the slogan. Genuine leaders know what this is all about, take it very seriously and put their heart and soul in their business. You know, the word heart is a sum of words and elements, as it were. Just imagine how many words you can make up with the letters of the word heart. It starts with the ear, the ear that you need to use to listen to others. What you do with your ear is to hear, that's the second word. And above all: listen to what is not being said, because we often listen without actually hearing anything. The third and possibly most important word to complete the 'heart' is art! That is, the art of transforming the things you've heard into things that matter to your customers.

The essence here is the art of making contact. Communication works the same way as electricity, electricity which you can generate. A good contact ignites the light to the heart, a bad contact first causes sparks and then short-circuiting. If you don't manage to make contact, you've lost 'them' forever. But if it works, you will have got the bliss. If you succeed in bending things towards being an ISP, the famous Inspirational Selling Point, your brand or 'thing' will win. That is to say, if you've put your heart into it and are perceived as a friend. Given that all conditions and offers are more or less identical, people will always prefer to buy from a friend. But also in case conditions and offers differ a bit, people will still go and buy things from friends first. That's why you always need to create a social brand personality, since a person can become a friend, but a cold and inanimate object never will: you need to matter.

A well-known case that shows us how you should handle these matters is the reset of Starbucks. Starbucks CEO Howard

Schultz said the following in one of his famous Starbucks keynote speeches: "If your absence doesn't make any difference, your presence won't either!" The brand had pretty much lost its way, but climbed back on top under his inspiring leadership. This also put a stop to the academic drivel regarding the subject of brand storytelling. Phrases like 'Starbucks is new and improved', 'Now with 50% more than the leading bla bla bla' were banished to the realm of make-believe by him. Consumers think this is uninteresting drivel, it bores them and quite honestly, they don't have the time for it. One day, Schultz closed all the Starbucks stores and pressed the reset button. He put the soul back into the body and literally put his heart in it. His philosophy was: if people don't come to our stores, it's not their fault. It is up to us to seduce them with the best coffee in the world. They need to want to hang out with us again, to chill.

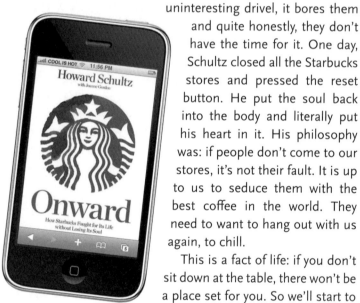

This is a fact of life: if you don't sit down at the table, there won't be a place set for you. So we'll start to set the table ten minutes before the store opens, as it were! You need to be and feel welcome. This is a feeling we all recognize. Feeling welcome is an emotional sensation, obviously, since you 'feel' something.

E specially in the food sector, this is the main ingredient in your marketing mix. Food equals emotion and this emotion evolves from global to local, from price to value, from healthy to energetic. From male to female and approachable; from plates full of food to smaller, tastier portions. As a matter of fact, this rule applies to all business sectors: leave out the word food and you have grabbed the art of the heart. Some people call it revitalizing, all of a sudden, but I prefer to call it soul power.

Why don't you decide to put your ear to the ground the consumers walk on, at least once every 100 days? And make sure you actually listen. Then you can put the words into action, immediately. Don't get taken by surprise, have a good time and start dancing with all your know-how. If you can't dance, don't blame the dance floor! Believe me, you can do it too. At present it isn't hard at all and it's often free, as well, if you use the social media! Remember: dance first, think later!

THE POWER OF 'RE': re connect and re earn! Just RESET your brain

Mike Ferrier

Think of What the 'Re' Can Do for You..

No, we're not talking about Do-Re-Mi here, but about the 're' for reset. When a computer gets stuck and you're in despair, the only thing left to do is to press the reset button. Without exactly knowing what you're doing, you can at least get all the processes to start from scratch. In the same way, the 're' may be or become an important stage in the ongoing competition for the customer's favor, as much for you as for anyone else. The reset strategy is also very safe, and it's often the first step you take, as safety is an important topic in the current technological world. As you know, the dark power of the Internet is increasingly abused by ever smarter people who will do anything to steal from you digitally. Although you won't be in too much trouble if you're essentially a safe haven, if you've built safety into your brand's DNA, because people like to do business with such a company.

With safety you can earn a lot of money. It is a real moneymaker, as certain software guys can confirm. A lot of them earn a very decent living on it. Since we're becoming more and more mobile by using our smartphones and iPads, that presents a great opportunity to strengthen the bond with your customers and attract some new ones. A whole new world of opportunities will open up. To reconnect often means that you can also re-earn, provided you can be trusted and therefore safe. Safety always comes first, because with all the new solutions ICT provides for mobile money transfers, the risk of fraud and theft is increasing too. In the next few years, the old-fashioned wallet will probably disappear altogether; in the near future, all payments and many other things will be dealt with via your cell phone. Maybe you only use your cell phone for paying for your parking space at the moment, but soon you'll also use it to pay for your groceries!

You can begin by studying these kinds of money transactions; it will give you a head start when things really take off. There is no doubt that these developments are going to continue, but the pace depends on the customer's wishes.

And the customer wishes a lot, as long as it makes life easier. The question of who is going to man the back offices still remains: Apple or Google? Or will it be left to the banks, such as Bank of America or J.P. Morgan? This could actually happen, although it all depends on the number of problems with electronic banking, which seem to have increased in the past year or so. There's also a possibility that some less obvious brands will emerge to handle this task; have you ever thought about providing this service yourself? Start thinking about it at an early stage, since you don't want to be overtaken by everybody else, like the bookshops. Biding your time is not an option in this age of technology, the battle for the customer's favor regarding financial services has already started. Hop on the bus as quick as you can and think about it. Don't 're' ject it! Because the 're' will simply continue, with or without you.

Business Happiness Is a Real Privilege...

Everything you do should feel good. Once you understand that doing business is just a game, you'll immediately start playing better. This applies equally to enterprising managers and to managing entrepreneurs; it all depends on how you see yourself. Of course you always play to win, with the whole team, with a clear goal in mind. Winners always have a plan, losers often only have excuses. Winners think in opportunities, losers in problems. Winners make things happen, losers wait until something happens, that sums up the philosophy of football coach Vince Lombardi. And it's true: your luck is not determined by the cards you've been dealt, but by how you play the cards you have.

You might very well be forced to make some unpopular decisions along the way, such as letting your best salesperson go. Or giving your best hitter a different job in order to give the rest of the team some breathing space. The coach of the Dutch national field hockey team recently decided not to select two of his best players; he deliberately cut down two giant oaks to give the rest of the forest more light, as it were. To let the others prove their worth and give them more air, so the team can grow. When you make such a decision you can expect the whole world to come down hard on you. Nobody in the sport of field hockey had ever thought this would happen; it was a truly revolutionary act to cut down those oaks. Nevertheless, the national coach stuck to his principles and so created a new reality. This new reality is much wilder than any fantasy, certainly in this case. Has he gone mad or does he foresee things we haven't yet noticed? The answer lies in the future, although this much is certain: "If you cannot do great things, do small things in a great way!" Cut down the biggest trees in the forest and you will get new energy to do what's necessary.

Huge, life-sized changes will surely be noticed by your customers, but by your competitors too, of course. They will be wasting their time, searching for a reason for your change of course, while in the meantime you can step on it and energetically strive for the business happiness you're entitled to. You've got a new story to tell, which people will listen to, the more so when they notice you have a clear goal in mind. Decisions regarding the staff are always a driving force behind innovations! As long as there is a logical explanation which you can make clear; it's all about what you do and, above all, why you do it. If your answer is that you're after business happiness, you'll get away scot-free. In the example mentioned above, the field hockey coach will also get away with it, once the Olympic gold medal has been won. Let's hope he manages to coach his energetic team to win this medal, otherwise

he'll be slaughtered by 16 million Dutch coaches who will never forgive him for his stupid decision. Even if it's a prerogative to be allowed to make decisions.

Who would you let go, to make room for new happiness? Forget about the emotions that surround such a step and don't be afraid of a bit of friction. Medals will only shine more because of it.

Facts, Fiction, Focus, and Above All: Fun!

Few things in life are 100% certain, except for this: you've almost finished reading *Cool is Hot*. Thank you very much for wanting to read the whole book. But the question is, what are you going to do with it? Each day is followed by a night. And after that, the sun rises again, no matter whether things are going great or not so great. At least that's 100% for sure.

That's why it's important to focus on the future and not to dwell on the past for too long. Be sure to be well-rested before you take the next step, and take it wisely. Never lie, because nowadays everything is fully transparent, the Internet forgets nothing.

Wise people will keep on creating more opportunities than there actually are, surprising us time and again with moments that really matter. Whether your name is Microsoft CEO Steve Balmer (watch his Gorilla dance on YouTube) or Barack Obama, who recently sang to his audience. His "I'm so in love with you" made the news in a staggering 150 countries.

Be inspired and always base yourself on the facts. If you focus on the goal you want to reach, you'll be allowed to dream on the basis of the fiction that is actually attainable. As far as that's concerned, you should always remain a realistic optimist, not a builder of castles in the air who has no credibility. It's impossible to squeeze 1.5 gallons out of a one-gallon tank; that's a fact. It's better to engage in a dialogue about the things you want to attain than to hold a monologue that lacks credibility.

Also, stop discriminating on the basis of age; the youngsters of Generation Z are already pretty smart, but don't forget to bring in the old hands and ask them for advice. You'll be amazed at their strength, resilience and especially their wisdom, which they'll gladly share with you.

Visit the keynote speeches of well-known, competent people more often, listen to them and open your filter. If you're ever so lucky as to be able to see and hear the famous Warren Buffet, then move heaven and earth to attend his speech. Check out YouTube for the speech he held in 1999 at the annual Allen & Company Sun Valley Conference, in which numerous outstanding businessmen, politicians and artists took part. And read his recent speech and interview in *Time Magazine*.

Many of his tips will make you a better person right away, because Warren Buffet believes in honesty and fairness! He believes you have to learn something before you start reaping the benefits, or as he puts it: "Learn before you earn." He also believes that you can make money, and that governments should make people's lives better by improving the infrastructure in such a way that everything feels better. But above all, he believes in happiness. Yes, in business happiness. That kind of happiness will only come your way if you believe in it. If you are willing to bet on this, make sure this message comes across to your audience, your employees or your colleagues. Use all kinds of theatrics and showmanship to make sure the story sinks in and is understood. So everybody will get a taste for it: you too. When you see the boss having fun, the spark will truly fly.

After all this, you'll take the journey towards the goal together. Get together at least 3 times a year and demonstrate the business goals. If you're not such a gifted speaker, then let somebody else tell the main story. But do the introduction yourself. You'll be amazed at what you can achieve by being authentic. Stay focused on your target; that's important, because your customers and your staff will reward you for it. Actually, you'll be making the shift from a planned economy to an economy of initiatives. Inspire people and encourage them to take action, this way you will always be a front-runner.

Naturally, you can also generate business by using fiction,

but it won't take the public long to see right through your stories. Unless, of course, you're active in the Scottish tourist industry, since Nessie, the Loch Ness monster, manages to surface each time business is a bit slow. And wham, the hotels are full again and everybody wants to catch a glimpse of her. No kidding. There's a business truth to be found in this monster legend: as long as you make sure you stay afloat, you'll be visible.

Don't wait until you drown, because before you know it they will have forgotten you. Nowadays, there are so many things that can seduce the public that you'll have to start pumping energy into your business (or brand, or company) right away, as soon as you feel bad times coming on. To make everybody laugh at the stunts you pull to make the moment of seduction, that is, Nessie, emerge again.

It's true that if you can't convince people, you can always seduce them. And you're allowed to put everything at stake here, because your main interest is happiness! Don't have doubts, because that's the moment you lose. Focus on winning and you will see: the win will come your way. JFDI!

...and it's about time!

One more thing – one last reflection, taken from Steve Jobs' world-famous speech:

"

Your time is limited, so don't waste it living someone else's life. Don't be trapped by dogma — which is living with the results of other people's thinking. Don't let the noise of others' opinions drown out your own inner voice. And most important, have the courage to follow your heart and intuition. They somehow already know what you truly want to become. Everything else is secondary.

"

Cool is Hot Glossary

100 Days Move	Divide the year into periods of 100 working days each, and introduce a clear goal for each period. To motivate and inspire.
1,000 Days Goal	Goal for the longer term. Every 100 days, the progress towards this goal is evaluated to check whether the company is still on course to attain its 1,000 Days Goal.
3"12"E rule	Attract attention within 3 seconds, make sure you are the chosen one within the next 12 seconds, and you will have secured the E for Eternity, although you need to have the E for Energy embedded in your DNA.
3 Rs	Redefine, Reinvent, Renew, also called the R factor. Keep re-inventing yourself all the time.
Agenda-setting	The influence of the media on the public; if anything is highlighted in the media, the masses will also pay attention to it.
AIDA 1.0	Antiquated, out-of-date marketing model; in an advertisement the following 4 steps should be addressed: Attention, Interest, Desire, and Action.
Appmania	The fad of developing an 'app(lication)' for each activity or task, which can be used on mobile devices such as the iPhone or the iPad.
Bliss	Heavenly, happy feeling. Make sure the customer experiences this.
B's rule	Be the best, not the biggest; as a result you will become the biggest, so let it be!
BtB	Business to Business, mutual business transactions between companies.
Business Happiness	Have fun doing business, establish pleasant contacts with customers and colleagues.

Center of Excellence	Internal expertise and innovation center. Every company needs one for developing new ideas.
CEO	Chief Executive Officer. In short, the boss.
CERN	Derived from the French *Conseil Européen pour la Recherche Nucléaire*, a European center for nuclear research, based in Switzerland.
CFO	Chief Financial Officer, in short: the main bookkeeper of the company. If you want to maintain a pleasant relationship with this person, call him or her the Chief Fun Officer.
Clicks and bricks	You click while ordering a product on the Internet, but if you actually go out into the real world and visit a store, you will be heading for the bricks, the stone building.
Comfort zone	The environment in which someone feels most comfortable. It is hard for everyone to step outside this zone.
Cool	Better than Great, and just as good as Hot.
CSI	Customer Satisfaction Index; this index is created by measuring customer behavior.
Defriend	Getting rid of superfluous or unwanted (girl) friends, who keep clinging to you through all kinds of social networks.
Desire	Consumer interest, the will to buy a product. Customers need to desire your brand, but also grant you the turnover.
DM (direct marketing)	Advertising products by approaching potential customers in a direct and personal way.
EEC	Energy, Enthusiasm, and Creativity; all necessary to excel as an entrepreneur.
EQ	Emotional intelligence; in future, decisions to purchase will increasingly be taken on the basis of EQ, on gut feeling, rather than on the rational IQ.
Evoked set	The well-known and favorite brands that are known to all consumers, and which spring to buyers' minds when they decide to buy something.

Generation Z	The young adults who will enter the workplace and take over the world around the year 2020, very familiar with apps and joined at the hip with all sorts of electronic equipment.
Hot	Hip, fashionable, trendy, far out: as an entrepreneur, this is what you aspire to.
Idea safari	Find inspiration with competitors, innovators, and innovative organizations.
Intuition	Intuition is reason coupled to rush; listen to your heart but also to your head, since they work together very fast.
IQ	Intelligence Quotient, a way of measuring someone's intelligence. Although increasingly, the decision to purchase is arrived at on the basis of emotions, see also EQ.
ISP	Inspirational Selling Point, which has replaced the USP. As an entrepreneur you need to inspire your customers, this way you will attract the crowd and conquer their hearts.
IT/ICT	Information (and Communication) Technology, this is what it's all about in the future.
Karmanomics	Doing business while inspired by Buddhist principles.
KISS	Keep it Stupid Simple, Keep it Simple, Stupid, or Keep it Smart & Simple, it's all about not making things too complicated if you want to be successful.
NAFTA	Now Ask For The Account: don't forget to ask whether you have really secured the deal, after each conversation.
Nerd	Also called geeks, goofs, or freaks: people who devote all their time to a single (computer) hobby, at which they're very good, but which also makes them a bit weird.
PAR	While applying the 3"12"E rule it is important to obtain the Primary Affective Reaction within the first 3 seconds, that is, the first impulsive, positive reaction of a customer.

Pay-Off Line	Slogan that characterizes a brand or a company, and which attracts customers.
PoC	Point of Contact, a spot in the brain where contact is made, without the person being aware of it.
Refuse attitude	A person with this attitude does not listen much to others, and is not open to the opinions of other people.
Retailer	Someone who sells things directly to the public, often in a shop.
ROI shift	A shift from the Return On Investment principle to the principle of Return On Involvement (get the customers involved), and finally, to the Return On Ideas, where creativity is rewarded by the customers.
SAR	Given the 3"12"E rule, the Secondary Affective Reaction is about the 12 seconds during which the customer reflects before deciding whether or not to buy the product.
Space-time continuum	The entirety of time and space in which we live; in Science Fiction TV series Star Trek they juggle this concept on a regular basis by letting people travel through time and explore whole new worlds and parallel dimensions.
SQ	Spiritual intelligence, the spirit that each company or brand needs to possess if it wants to attract customers. At the moment, the basis of buying behavior is shifting from the IQ to the EQ, and then on to the SQ.
SSS	Speed, service, and smile, they lead to success.
Head - heart - wallet	The road to the customer's favor goes via the head, the heart, and then the wallet.
TOBA	Top of Brand Awareness, the degree to which customers are aware of a brand.
TOPA	Top of Person Awareness, the degree to which customers are aware of the personality of a designer, a company, or a brand.

Twitter	An online medium which allows you to send a message of up to 140 characters, by cell phone, tablet, or computer.
USP	Unique Selling Point, an old marketing concept that says that as a company, you need to distinguish yourself by offering something unique to your customers.
Viral	A marketing technique that uses social networks to enhance the fame of a brand, a kind of mouth-to-mouth advertising on the Internet.
Vlog	A video blog, which is a video log or diary on the Internet, where the story is told by means of a video.
Web care	Maintaining customer contact through the Internet, especially via the social media.
WWSD	What Would Steve Do? What would Apple's Steve Jobs have done in this case? Great question, the answer teaches you a lot.
X-files	Popular SF TV series from the 1990s, in which the main characters Mulder and Scully have to contend with extraterrestrials and other mysteries.